Tales from a Nobody

G.C. Cook

This book is dedicated to my daughter, Makenna, who has this future in front of her. The poor sap.

I would also be remiss if I didn't dedicate this book to my ex-wife, for without her and her attorney, none of this would be necessary.

Contents

A Note from The Guy Who Wrote This

This book, if we can call it that, is a work of fiction. Many moments mirror experiences I had growing up, but as my friends and family can attest, I have hugely embellished these stories in the retelling for my own and (hopefully) your amusement. I have always been a firm believer in not letting the truth get in the way of a good story.

The book is meant to represent the viewpoint of a narrator during his teens. Hopefully I have been able to capture some of the wonder that I believe the time when we are growing-up gives us. In order to tighten up the story, I have had to take multiple characters and build them into one. Megan, in particular, is a combination of some of the feelings I had towards several girls and really represents some of the challenges that I have seen people in my life go through. Believe it or not, I have also had more than three friends in my life, though not by much, and I have smashed some of their grotesque characteristics into a few likenesses that are very sorry, indeed. Consider it artistic license.

I have also painted the characters of the narrator's parents with an interesting brush. This is, after all, a work of fiction, but I did take some of my old recollections and life experience and try to build interesting characters from the viewpoint of a teenager who doesn't think he cares about what his parents are up to, but of course is deeply affected by them. In order to do this, I built two parents who seemed to be dealing with a divorce in very different ways. I wanted to build them in the judgmental way a teenager seems to view his parents. At least I was always pretty righteous in my judgments as a teenager. To this end, I wanted to create flawed parents in both the narrator's and the readers' eyes. Hopefully I created two interesting characters as well. The narrator clearly idolizes his father and may gloss over his faults. His mother he tends to demonize more as she is the day-to-day authority figure. Hopefully her true care for him comes through in a few key moments in the book. It is his mother, in her own way, who is there to pick up the pieces. For me, these characters were the most difficult and important in the book as they are the stabilizing force in our lives as teens. I hope I did that justice.

I want to thank a few people. First, my parents for without them this book would not be possible. A long time ago my father challenged me to write a book and fifteen years later I did. I can't control if anyone reads it, but this was a promise I made to the both of us. I am sure he shook his head at many moments of it. My mother is where I picked up my flair for drama and nurtured this with musicals and with her borderline abusive use of Dionne Warwick sing-alongs on car trips.

My friend Mike also inspired this tale. A few years ago, he wrote a book and asked me to read it. After I finished it I turned to my wife and proclaimed, "I can do that." So I did. Throughout the process, he has been an ear to bounce ideas off of. So this book is basically his fault, and I take no responsibility for it.

There were countless people who read this or heard my ideas over the years and politely listened. I owe Joe, Tara, Trevor, Mike, Leslie and many others – thanks for listening. If you were one of them, please assume I mean you.

I want to thank Leslie, in particular, for her help editing this book. She has been pushing me to do this the best it can be done. She has spent hours on all aspects. I cannot thank her enough for her belief in me and my, can we call it, voice?

This is like the story I should have told my therapist the first time. And like most stories, it seems, it starts and ends with a girl.

Prologue

Everyone dreams of growing up to be somebody – a great actor or athlete, a doctor who cures cancer, or a super-agent who saves the world from terrorist gangrene attacks. Everyone dreams of having fame and fortune, being suave and good looking like, say, Drew Carey.

But here's the problem: if everyone is somebody who is going to be nobody?

Not everyone can be somebody. Somebody needs to be a nobody, like the adult movie theater janitor, deodorant tester, or Sumo wrestler uniform adjuster. Somebody has to be the nobody that kind of gets the girl or almost makes the big catch. The world is built on the backs of nobodies; you just don't know it because somebody didn't tell you about them.

This is the story of one such nobody who wanted to be somebody and (perhaps) can relate to everybody. This is the story of a nobody who was transfixed by somebody, who dreamt of falling in love with everybody but whose heart was stolen by somebody – and nobody understood it. For a nobody knows a nobody even if somebody doesn't notice how much he loves somebody.

Did you get all that? This is nobody's story. In other words, my story.

Nobody

There was a man who sat each day on the Seattle waterfront. On a sign he had written, "I am blind, wet and poor." It was Seattle; it rained often. Every day people would walk by him and yet no one would drop money in his cup. No matter the weather, the sign remained the same, "I am blind, wet and poor."

Now it so happened that a woman walked by this man each day and took notice of the sign, so she asked, "Sir, today is a beautiful day. The sun is out and life is good. Why do you have such a depressing sign?"
"What do I know of sun and warmth?" he responded. "I am blind and I am cold. I have never seen the sun."

So the woman sat with him and in great detail painted the picture of the mighty sun with her words. Each day from then on she would stop and explain the scene in front of him: the crisp blue of the water, the warm glow of the sunrise. In response to her kindness he would describe in great detail the sharp smell of the sea air and the sweet song of the birds. And in time the man could see, for the woman became his eyes. In time the woman could truly hear as the man had taught her to listen.

One day as the woman sat next to the man she noticed the sign had changed. It now read, "I may be blind, but I can see a beautiful day." The woman quietly smiled at the change. As people walked by and took notice of his joy they were overcome with the desire to be a part of the happiness. Within the hour the cup was full.

   -- *As told by Jack Lock, teacher, coach, and friend.*

The Phone Call

It was late at night, perhaps on a weekend, I don't recall for sure. I remember a small storm blustered outside; hours earlier my young daughter had crawled into our bed, afraid of the rage of noise outside her window.

Once I had settled back into sleep, a phone call woke me. It was on my cell phone, which rested next to my bed lest I miss a Groupon coupon in the middle of the night.

The number was blocked and read only, "Private Network." When I picked up the receiver all I heard was the jagged breathing of another soul.

"Hello?" I asked.

Nothing but the breath followed by the click of an empty line. I thought nothing of it and tried to drift back into sleep. It could have been minutes or seconds or hours but again the phone rang. Again the number was private.

"Hello?!" I answered, with a terse edge this time.

The other end was just hollow breathing followed by the click.

Frustrated now, I sat up in bed, and seconds later the number appeared again on the phone as the ringer shuddered.

"Okay, who is this!?"

Quietly, a feminine voice recited my name.

"Yes," I responded.

Quiet sobs pulsed through the line. They were so subtle I may have missed them, except my mind was working along with the voice on the line. I could see a woman with dark hair hunched over a phone, her back to me. I could see the sobbing movement from her shoulders. Abruptly, the call ended.

Slightly spooked, I let my mind race. Who would be making these calls? A family member, perhaps, but I doubted anyone that close to me would hesitate to tell me what was going on. Was I being stalked? That would be pretty cool, actually…

As I let my mind wander, the phone rang again.

"Hello," I said, softly this time, hoping to convey compassion.

"I'm sorry," whispered the soft voice from a million miles away. She was deeply buried inside herself. I could feel her loss of confidence through the receiver.

"Don't apologize. Do you need help?"

"Not any more. I just wanted to hear your voice."

A pause as her breath took a jagged edge.

"Do you ever wonder what may have been? You ever just think about all the mistakes you've made and wonder, if only it had gone a different way?"

"No, not really."

"I do. I wonder if the sum of all my choices led me to this place in life, or was I destined to be here? It never mattered what I did to try and stop it, I was going to burn the village, you know?"

11

As she finished the sentence I could hear the phone being wrestled away from her. A male voice firmly demanded the phone. She whispered into it, "I'm sorry. I shouldn't have called."

She was gone. I was puzzled. I looked at my sleeping daughter and wife and thought about what she said. I had made many choices, but they led me here and this is where I wanted to be. I had no regrets, just happy memories. It made me sad that not everyone felt the contentment that I did. I guess that makes me one of the lucky ones.

Spin the Bottle

When I was twelve years old I knew I would be great with women. An epic event occurred that convinced me that not only was I a very desirable member of the opposite sex, but I was also destined for greatness in the field of lovemaking. The event in question was a game of Spin the Bottle.

Meet Katie, Megan, and Laura, the three most desirable seventh graders that my small Catholic school had to offer. Somehow, I found myself in Laura's basement one weekday afternoon, receiving my first kiss.

It all started simply enough. After school I rode my bike home, and along the way I ran into the three girls after they got off the "Orange" bus route they all took home every day. Sometimes I took that bus route too, so I may or may not have been well aware of just when they got dropped off and may have happened to be in the exact same spot when it occurred. Then again, maybe not. It was years ago and it's all a little hazy now. Nevertheless, the girls, probably feeling obligated because I was following them, invited me to Laura's house.

Moments later I found myself in the basement with the three girls staring at me. I am not sure whose idea it was to play Spin the Bottle but I, for one, did not object. In retrospect, I wish I could talk to the girls and find out why I was the one that was picked to be every one's first kiss. I was not a popular guy, so there was nowhere my status could go but up. Actually, if anything, it could knock me down a social peg or two. At least that was what the girls in college would tell me. I don't think I had great looks or was a great social wit. My guess is that I was the nice guy who happened to be in front of them at the time a hormone sprung loose. For me it was the best luck I would have with women for many, many years.

13

Laura didn't have a bottle; in the early 90s soda bottles were not a prevalent item. We tried spinning a Coke can but that lacked any real momentum behind its revolutions. Next we tried a remote control, but that seemed awkward and clunky (much like me). We finally settled on a French's mustard bottle that we found in the garage fridge. It was two years past its expiration, so it was perfect.

The circle lacked any true circular definition as the girls huddled as a group on one side of the room and I faced them. Laura spun first, and the bottle pointed at Megan. There was a flaw in the concept of the game. As the only guy in the room, her spinning was a matter of semantics rather than chance. She simply had to kiss me. The spin was an exercise in futility. She leaned over the circle and closed her eyes, rocked on the heels of her palms, and moved in closer for the kiss. I sat there, stunned and afraid. I assume I had the same look that an antelope may have moments before he is culled from the pack – utter terror.

Just as she was about to brush my lips with hers she screamed and fell back. She couldn't bring herself to kiss me. This, I was emotionally prepared to handle. The idea of a girl not being able to bring herself to kiss me was an idea I could wrap my mind around. In fact, it would be a common feeling in the future. What happened next, however, was not. Too nervous to kiss me, Laura recoiled back to her haunches. Megan was the one who came up with the great idea.

"Just kiss him," she said to Laura.

"No, I can't," said Laura.

"Well, what if we both kiss him at the same time?" Megan said.

What a great idea! The girls leaned in and both planted a wet kiss on a cheek, my first and only threesome. The current that went through my body was unreal. My first kiss, and it was with not one, but *two* girls.

We continued playing the game, all three girls taking their turns. When I left that autumn night it was dark and the street lights were making shadows on the asphalt. I rode that Schwinn of mine back home as fast as I could. The adrenaline coursing through my body allowed me to pedal a power and speed that rivaled a fully doped Lance Armstrong. As the weeks went on, I would often join Laura, Katie and Megan in that glorious basement. Not only that, but I got a bit of a reputation with the ladies. I was the first kiss of most of the girls in that little class in that little Catholic school. Often the kiss was stolen at school during a recess or just after class in the park under a large swaying tree. Each time it was electric and special. Nothing, however, compared to being in that basement – just me and the three most beautiful girls I knew.

After one game of Spin the Bottle, I walked home with Katie and Megan. Megan was spending the night at Katie's, and since Katie lived only a few blocks from me, we decided to walk home together. I held hands with Katie and Megan walked beside us with my bike in tow. At the end of the block, Katie and I kissed under the street lamp. It was only dusk but it was already dark and cold, so the roads felt private. Megan startled me as we stopped at the next street lamp. I leaned in for a kiss, and after its conclusion she asked, "Do you want to be my boyfriend?"

"I guess," I said, and then I switched back to Katie.

Inside, though, I was elated. Megan was beautiful. She had strawberry blond hair with sparkling blue eyes. She had a deep laugh and a powerful smile. She lit up rooms. Her eyes could dance with life. And here she was asking me to be her boyfriend – her *first* boyfriend. I knew there would be plenty of boyfriends in her life, but I was the first.

When we all arrived at the next street lamp (after a block's worth of a walk), we prepared to make the exchange back to Megan. It was as this exchange was made that Megan broke the news to me: we were breaking up. I guess we had been drifting apart for several driveways. My first relationship lasted only a city block.

Megan would grow to have men throw themselves at her. She knew how to play the strings of their hearts; she knew how to make them feel special (and defeated all at the same time).

She and I lost touch after high school, only to reconnect shortly before my 20th birthday. She learned that no one was throwing me a party, and even though she had only reconnected with me a few days before, she called every mutual friend she could find, and found a way to break into my apartment to set up the party. When I returned home the house was decorated and festive, and she was at the blender making daiquiris. This was the Megan that men fell in love with. She made you feel like the world revolved around you. This beautiful girl was once again making me feel important.

As the night wore on, I sat with her and thanked her for the party. I was hoping she did this for me – not because she saw me as a friend who needed some cheering up on his birthday, but because she saw me as someone she wanted to be with. Instead, I learned she would be leaving the following week to go back to Los Angeles to be an actress. I did my best to live in the moment of the party, although it would be the last time I would see those eyes dance.

Megan went to L.A., where it all went wrong. She had a boyfriend who told her he knew all the right people there. She was young and funny and beautiful, so there's no way she could fail in the big city. But when she arrived, she learned that he didn't know anybody. In addition to being beautiful, Megan was also very naïve. The boyfriend got her hooked up with the wrong crowd. The crowd was deep into drugs and parties. She had thought that if she was on the fringes maybe someone in this crowd would help her realize her dream of being a model or an actress. In the end, all she realized was a dependency on drugs.

So she slunk back home and hid. She tried to shake the habit but found herself sinking deeper into despair. Her strawberry blond hair became ratty and thin. She dyed it black. Her body became thin and bony and unattractive. The greatest loss was her eyes – they had once sparkled with innocence and laughter but were now filled with a murky darkness. Her eyes would never be the same. Maybe that's what a lifetime does to you. Maybe my eyes are dull. I saw her eyes years later as she was working to pull her life together and learned that I missed them. The ghost of her beauty was still there. The woman who had never had a shortage of boys throwing themselves at her was all alone. I hoped the right guy would come along and make those eyes dance again.

But I digress…

We became better at Spin the Bottle. Then Mike, one of my best friends, decided he wanted to take some of the chance out of it. It was my birthday and we were going to throw a dance party in my basement. That Saturday afternoon, Mike came over to help set up a plan. He was forced to let his little sister, Krissy, tag along. She sat in the back and quietly did whatever girls younger than me did to keep from being bored. I didn't care what she did. She was a sixth grader, so she didn't exist to me.

"We need some order to this game," Mike said.

I suggested an alternative. "I heard about a better game, 'Seven Minutes in Heaven.' I guess it's pretty cool. A boy and a girl go into a room and do 'whatever' for seven minutes."

"Too risky," Mike replied. "There is no guarantee that you will be allowed to make out. We need more guarantees, not less. Why don't we combine that with 'Truth or Dare?' Then they have to go into the room for seven minutes and we dare them to make out."

"Maybe," I said, "but what if they take truth? That doesn't help us."

"Right, the game is just Dare. Better yet, let's make a schedule. We have three rooms so let's schedule everyone to a time slot."

So that's what we did. We took a whiteboard and we made a list, placing each girl with a guy in one of three rooms. If we liked you, you got a room with Megan, Katie or Laura. If we didn't, it was Ursula or Tabitha. As always, we fought for who would get more time with Megan. Krissy brought up the point that Megan may prefer to go into Seven Minutes in Heaven with her boyfriend, Danny. We told Krissy to shut the fuck up. What does a sixth grader know anyhow? She just rolled her eyes at us.

The party didn't go according to schedule. It started well, but Megan eventually caught on to the fact that she was never going to be out of a room one way or the other. If she wasn't going for the schedule, then no girl would. We had to

18

improvise, and this meant we went back to the old standby: the bottle.

Over time, the bottle disappeared as we gained more confidence. Eventually, girls would just come over, and we would find a way to thin the herd until we found ourselves alone with someone. More often than not, I found myself with Katie.

Katie was cute. She had curly brown hair, green eyes, olive skin and a warm nature. She lived just a few blocks from me and I would often sneak out of my house at night and tap on her window. She would meet me and we would kiss in the park under the moon, or walk among the silent streets holding hands.

Back then, midnight felt like the most sacred and quiet time in the world. The adrenaline rush that poured through us as we held hands was better than any drug. Katie was kind to me, but there was a problem – she wasn't mine alone.

That fat bastard, Fucking Walsh, had laid claim to her as well – and he had home field advantage since he lived next door. In order to see her more and counter Fucking Walsh's home field advantage, I did the only thing I could think of: I became her paper boy. And as it turned out, Walsh's. (Although during my tenure they never received a paper – after all, all is fair in love and war.)

I could feel Katie starting to slip away, so Mike came up with an idea: I would fight Fucking Walsh and claim Katie as my prize when I defeated him. It was perfect. I challenged him to a fight after school (or, perhaps I should say, Mike challenged him on my behalf.) Everyone showed up, even the girls.

The fight lasted all of one minute. I lost. Katie left with Walsh and I picked my teeth up off the ground. I sat all alone in defeat and vowed that I would avenge the loss. Katie would be mine.

The only person that remained to help me home was Krissy. She had followed Mike to see the fight too. She gave me my book bag and handed me my rusted out old Schwinn. She didn't say anything, but it was reassuring that someone was there to hear me as I proclaimed, "I will have revenge." She shook her head in disgust.

Living in this Moment

Growing up, you naturally fall into a social circle. A lot of it is determined by chance – the neighborhood you grow up in or the school you attend – but it will prove to be a defining factor in your growth as a person. Who knows who we could become if we were surrounded by the right peers? Sure, we may all eventually fall into the right career, but how hard is the path to get there? How much easier is it if the right support group pushes us and picks us up?

For those of you who know boys becoming teenagers, you know there is no such thing as peer support. There is only pain, ridicule and more pain. For most young men it seems important to take the hurt that others subject on them and bury it down deep inside where no one can get to it, then take that pain and hurt and remain silent until their late teens when they erupt in a hormone-induced rage that results in a terrible blog with an accompanying YouTube channel

I suppose they could talk to loved ones about their fears and anger and try to work it out, but in the young man's paradigm, that would make you a pussy and girls don't like pussies and if girls don't like you, you have no standing with your pack of friends. Having no standing with your pack of friends makes you a loser that no one wants to be around, and we end up right back at the YouTube channel with only likes from your aunt Ethel and an Indian Uber driver named Raj from Newark (who, incidentally, has more likes on his channel). Either way you're fucked from a social standing perspective.

I was a chunky kid as a youth. In my early learning years I also had a pretty obvious speech impediment and was unable to pronounce my Rs . This distracted kids from my weight gain, but there was always plenty of fuel for a character roast.

Even years later at my wedding, Andrew, a grade school friend, told everybody that he thought I was special – special in the way in which a kid wears a helmet and oven mitts and is best friends with an imaginary, cape-wearing gerbil. It was a riveting toast. He felt guilty about it and thought it may have affected our friendship, so he repeated the toast at another friend's wedding a few years later.

Boys are like dogs; they run in packs – wild, unmanageable packs. My pack was as follows:

- **Mike**: self-proclaimed alpha-dog and the first person to get drunk, smoke a cigarette and finger an ugly girl until she had a distinct limp.
- **Dan**: the real alpha-dog who was good looking, athletic, and charming. Every girl loved him. We loved him because he could hold his booze as a sixth grader.
- **Andrew**: the lawyer's son. He could argue his way out of trouble, but usually just hit people.
- **James**: nicknamed "Fucking Walsh" because every time you started to talk about him it was about something stupid he had done. For example, "Oh man, Fucking Walsh tried to light his dog's balls on fire again, and now the dog has third-degree burns and needs to be put to sleep." James was always fighting with me for social status in the pack.
- **Me**: chubby and awkward, but my parents had a nice house with a pool and a full liquor cabinet – important social considerations.

As you can tell, all members of the pack played a role in our success and survival. Dan was the athletic leader; Mike was the diplomat. He was the most self-assured of the pack.

Andrew was the brute strength, F-ing Walsh the comic relief, and I provided the booze.

The first time we all drank together was the afternoon of a seventh grade baseball game. The game was at 5:00 pm., just a few short blocks from my house. Mike decided it would be a good idea to get drunk, then ride our bikes to the game. Dan agreed, so we had no choice but to follow or be left for dead in this lonely and dangerous social jungle.

When we got to my house Mike selected a fine bottle of Cutty Sark Scotch Whiskey. The smell was enough to gag a horse. We needed a mixer. We had two options: club soda or orange Tang. We obviously chose Tang. Scotch and Tang. It went down like a ten year-old on Father Flannigan – reluctant and with teeth. It was awful. We all took our drinks and Mike poured us another. After three of these we were feeling the effects. Then F-ing Walsh threw up. It was everywhere. We decided to leave for the game before anyone else hurled.

We rode our bikes towards the park like soldiers on a mission. Dan had his bat on his shoulder and we all had our gloves in our back waistband. There was a shortcut that went across a windswept bluff covered in snake grass. On this bluff trail, a now fully intoxicated Andrew lost his balance and flung himself (and his bike) fifty or so feet down the side of the trail. He could have been dead which seemed, of course, hysterical at the time. When Andrew came out of his concussed state he found it incredibly difficult to get up and get back on his bike. So, naturally, we left him behind. The game would start in just fifteen minutes, and we didn't want to be late.

As luck would have it, I was slated to pitch and F-ing Walsh was catching. Coach liked it when I pitched because I was too fat and slow to play any real positions. I wasn't very good when I was sober; but I was a real treat to watch when I was hammered. As the game started I reared backed, looked off what appeared to be multiple F'ing Walshes and hurled the ball at the middle one, hoping for the best.

The glory of baseball is it can take an unusual turn. In many ways baseball is like life. Success is measured in moments. The greatest to play the game still fail to hit the ball 70% of the time. In life, even the most successful of us fall flat on our face more often than we succeed. The beauty is that our minds are good at flushing all the failure and just keeping the warm memory of the positive successes. We are motivated both by that success and the fear of failing. Most of us can rationalize that failure and somehow spin it in a positive way. Good for you, but you still failed. Don't ever forget most of the time you are a horrible wretched pile of failure and everyone knows it. You're actually a train wreck – but good for you for trying.

Baseball is the same way. For much of my athletic career, I was a failure. I don't run well, I don't have very good coordination, and I have almost zero confidence. But that day, with the power of Scotch and Tang in my body, I was flush with great confidence. I owned that mound. I was bending that ball over the back of the plate. Kids swung in a futile fashion. I didn't normally have an A-game, but I did that day. I plowed through the line-up. I was untouchable. Even when they did get the bat on the ball it seemed to always find the soft hands of Dan (our inimitable shortstop), who was sobering up. I was not much of a hitter, but when I got my hips into it I could put a charge into a ball. In my first at bat I ripped a double down the first base line. This scored Dan from second. After the second inning we led 1-0.

This score held true until the fifth inning. After my powerful hit I was walked intentionally twice. The coach of our opponent was muttering something about me as I walked past his dugout. Something about "where the hell did this kid come from." He had me confused with a real athlete, which I relished. It was the first and last time that would ever happen and I was going to make the most of it.

To make things even better, Megan, Katie, and Laura had all made it to the game to watch. I found it tough to keep my bleary eyes off of Megan. Not only did she look shamefully radiant in her little halter-top and shorts but also I learned during the third inning that she had shaved her legs and armpits just for me. That is sexy shit, as I'm sure you know.

As the sixth inning began, I could feel my moment upon me. The surge of confidence ran through my rotund body. With each big pitch my teammates would chant my name and the coach would marvel at my skills. I had a blaze of determination in my eyes. I could not and would not be stopped. This was my game. I would not be denied. <Insert primal scream here.>

But like so many men before me, it all came crashing down. At the top of the seventh inning, the last inning of the game, I found myself looking at the sign from the catcher – and I was stone cold sober. Not only did I have all my wits about me, but I was no longer nauseous or suffering from cold sweats. Shit! I quickly called my infield onto the mound for a strategy conference.

"Shit guys, I don't think I can do this."

"What are you talking about?" asked F-ing Walsh.

"I am sober, man, there's no way I can do this sober."

"Damn, that sucks," said Captain Obvious (formerly known as Mike).

Coach Hughes walked out of the dugout to inquire what all the fuss was about.

Mike yelled, "Get back in the dugout – this has nothing to do with you, old man."

Coach Hughes raised his palms up, shrugged, and slunk back to the dugout, rolled a fresh cigarette and lit up. He rarely felt like coaching anyhow, so he was content sitting in the dugout on a nice summer afternoon. This allowed him some peace and quiet that he didn't have at home with his wife, whom he was convinced was trying to kill him by adding small traces of saltpeter to his food so he would be sterile and eventually die of sexual starvation. He figured he was just fine because he hadn't had a sexual thought about her since the last day of his honeymoon when he first heard her fart in her sleep. Frankly, he found the saltpeter a relief.

I returned to the mound, my confidence abolished. I scanned the crowd and my eyes fell upon Megan. Her smile gave me strength. I whirled back and threw the first pitch. It had nothing on it. It was blistered off the bat towards first. Andrew snagged it with a tremendous backhand and quickly stepped on the bag.

"I can do this," I told myself.

The next batter stepped into the box and found himself quickly down 0-2. On my third pitch I slipped off the mound and fell over. I chucked the ball up in desperation. It climbed into the air higher and higher until it looked like it might float into a cloud. As it hurtled back towards the earth, Walsh settled under it, and the batter wound up, his tongue hanging from the side of his mouth as he prepared to crush the ball. As he pulled his bat into the zone he failed to recognize that Walsh had moved up onto the plate to catch the ball. His bat found the soft part of Walsh's skull and knocked Walsh, his mask, and the ball about five feet from the dish. Stunned, the runner stood there until the ump told him to run. I pounced on the ball and whipped it to first.

Out. Two down, one to go for my first ever win, and hopefully, the heart of Megan.

It was at this point that things completely fell apart. I was tired, my head hurt, and my arm was sore. I eyed Megan again and she looked beautiful, much too beautiful for a fraud like me. Her blonde hair fell onto the soft tan skin of her shoulders and danced about in the breeze. From my perch on the mound I could hear the tones of her giggle – such sweet music.

One more to go, just one more out and it would be over. I pulled my weight back and channeled the power through my legs, up my core, and out my arm. I slung that ball for everything I had and it shot out as though from a cannon. It was as hard as I had ever thrown.

The batter swung, and as the ball crossed the zone it met the sweet, fat part of the bat. The concussion from the impact ricocheted off the walls of the small park. The ball just kept rising and rising and rising until it had no need to go any further. It was gone. The score was tied. I felt a huge weight fall onto my shoulders; I felt as if my back might break from the weight. Out walked Coach Hughes; Dan ran up to me but not before telling coach to walk back to the dugout. Coach did as he was told and happily strolled back, counting on his next cigarette.

"We're gonna win this game," Dan said "Just one more out. You can do this."

"I'm tired," I said. "I can't do this, look at what happened last time."

"That was just a moment and it has passed. Question is – what can you do in *this* moment? Live in this moment."

With inspirational wisdom dispensed, he trotted back to shortstop. He was right. Just one pitch.

I hefted back and sure enough, on the first pitch the batter swung and drove it into the ground. It skipped once, then twice and found Dan at shortstop.

He plucked it out of his mitt and fired to first. Beat him by three steps. Great play. Dan made those all the time. On a field, there was nothing he couldn't do.

As fate would have it, the bottom of the inning came down to me. Dan was on second base after a lead-off single. He stole second, but both Mike and Andrew struck out. F-ing Walsh had a hole in his head and was trying to walk to the hospital. His mother wouldn't allow him in the car because she didn't want any bloodstains on her rich Corinthian leather.

Then Dan's words rang through my head: "Live in this moment."

With the game on the line, Megan sat on her palms in the stands. Her bare shaved legs were swinging from the bench back and forth in nervous tension. In that moment I was as capable as any man who had ever stood at a plate. In that moment I would succeed. I may have failed in the past, but that was then – this is now. I could do this.

The first pitch sailed by me for a ball. "Good eye!" yelled Coach Hughes in a lame attempt to rationalize his lack of coaching to this point.

It had nothing to do with my eyes. I was too petrified to swing. "I can do this," became my mantra.

Next pitch. I swung from my heels and corkscrewed myself into the ground. Strike one. I wasn't even close.

The next pitch was high, but I couldn't help myself. I flung myself at it. Another miss. Strike two.

I pulled myself out of the box shaking my head in desperation, trying to pull myself together. I could feel sweat bead on my spine and channel itself down my back. It felt cold. I looked at Megan. She was striking in the sun. It was as if she was floating; or maybe I was just delirious with fear.

No. I could do this. In this moment, this pitch, I could do this. It occurred to me that this is very much like life. How many times have I stepped into the box and failed? To win you have to muster the guts to step back up to the plate, to be willing to face the failure and swing again. I could do this. I *would* do this.

As the pitch came in I locked in on it. My swing was easy, the power transferred from my hips to the bat. The ball bolted off of the bat and sailed over the second baseman. I ran towards first in my awkward gait, and Dan had already rounded third as I neared the bag.

He scored. We won! I had pitched the whole game. I made the game-winning hit. The team ran out of the dugout and mobbed...Dan.

I stood at first and wondered where *my* attention was. "Hey fuckers, I'm the one who won the game!" I thought. But I got nothing.

I saw Megan standing and clapping excitedly. I ran up the bleachers grabbed her shoulders and pressed my lips to hers as hard as I could. I could feel my skull grind on her skull. Ouch, too hard, ease up, live in the moment, don't head-butt the moment. I was slightly shocked as she kissed back. When we parted she smiled at me. The team was (finally) chanting for me to come down.

But by then it was too late. I couldn't move. I pressed my legs together and sat down, hoping nobody could see my reaction to that kiss.

Then as I looked up from my bleacher seat, I couldn't help but notice how smooth Megan's armpits were.

My First Date

The first time a girl was really caught in the web that is my charm was at a high school football game in the eighth grade.

It was Katie and she was lovely. She was built like a porcelain doll, and she had olive-colored skin, big green eyes and sweeping brown hair that seemed to wrap around her soft features. Her dark hair played well off her complexion, but nobody noticed because she had big boobs (at least for an eighth grader). I'm just guessing here, I didn't have a lot of experience in knowing what was normal vs. abnormal for a woman's development. To be honest, I still don't really know.

While we both attended All Saints, her family was poor compared to mine – that is to say their ski condo was shared with another family. To me, it seemed that dating her would be very much like a modern version of Romeo and Juliet (sans the tights and overall beauty of the male lead).

Allow me to set the stage for you...

The football stadium at the Jesuit high school in our hometown was the gathering spot for all local Catholic kids on fall Friday nights. While the much older (and obviously cooler) high school students crushed up against one another in the stands at the 50-yard line, the younger crowd milled about the edges at the desolate 20-yard line.

For a thirteen-year-old, the thrill and freedom of Friday nights was just about the best thing going. All my friends gathered in the stands while parental supervision was at a true minimum. One father, maybe two, would be sitting high up the bleachers, busy drinking whiskey out of a flask and watching the game with a vacant stare. You can always tell the stare of a pre-teen's parent. It's a thousand-yard stare like that of a homebound soldier; "I have seen some shit man, I have seen some shit."

These Friday nights became a ritual and a rite of passage. We would find our buddies and circle around, nervously eying the girls. It was very cliquish. Schools and genders did not intermingle. A head nod to a rival male would be the maximum allowable interaction. As for the girls, they were the targets. Pretty and innocent looking, they would stand like a herd of gazelles, some only slightly more attractive. The goal was always to charm one of these foreign girls into your control and hopefully find yourself alone with them. There was a rumored story where one boy had managed to pick off one of the herd and took her behind the bleachers and felt her breasts, but there has never been an eyewitness to confirm this. In fact, in the one hundred or so recorded years of Friday night football, no person has even risked breeching the chasm between the huddled groups to attempt a conversation with a girl. Most believed it would never happen in their lifetime.

It was a typical cold and dreary Friday night. There was a light frost on the field and a mist circled the stadium. It was too cold to brave the elements without a coat, so I was unable to properly show off my guns for the ladies. "Guns" or "pipes" are well-developed arms, not weapons. This can be misconstrued in some places, like Texas.

On this night the wind gusted in spastic bursts and whipped up leaves from the nearby park, providing an audible crunching under our sneakers. The lights were bright and the band played "Smoke on the Water" in a constant loop.

All the boys gathered together in a circle pausing only to allow an approved member of the pack in. Occasionally someone would throw their eyes over to search the faces of the girls before putting his head back into the circle and reporting back on the shape, size, and attire of whatever girl may have caught his eye. During a long-winded gust something happened that shook us to the very core. It was still early in the first quarter when from just outside the circle came an odd, high-toned voice. It was a girl from All Saints, and, oddly, she was calling my name. The circle opened leaving me exposed to three well-groomed young ladies. I am man enough to admit I was terrified.

The coven of little women stood in front of me. One, the ring leader, was rotund and tall with greasy brown hair that stuck together in clumps. She would pull at the tangled mess with her chubby hands and push it from her muddled brown eyes. She wore jeans that stretched over her protruding belly like the linen on a drum.

Next to the ring leader stood a dazzling blond who had light features, pale eyes and hair that curled just right to frame her face. We had all noticed her before. Her name was Carissa. Next to Carissa stood a small, thin brunette with thick glasses and one eyebrow where two belonged. The three sent chills up my spine as they beckoned me with their fingers to approach them.

"What is it?" I stammered, trying to play it cool.

"We have a message from Katie," the fat one said. She chewed her words. I was somewhat surprised a Chicken McNugget didn't try to escape from her mouth. Every time I had seen her she was eating. And true to form, she had a jumbo bag of M&M's in her hand.

"Katie?" I stammered. "That one over there?" I nervously pointed in Katie's general direction.

"Yes, that Katie. You know – you sit next to her at school," the rotund one said. In unison they threw their heads back and cackled in a high pitched tone. Somewhere several dogs yelped in pain.

"What…what…what does Katie want from me?"

I looked for some support from the young men around me but they seemed too entranced by the coven to rush to any form of support. The exception was Andrew, who was obliviously eating a candied apple and watching the game. He had made it clear he had no interest in girls and preferred to focus on more meaningful things like football and blowing shit up with left-over fireworks.

"Katie," the fat one spit, "has asked if you would like to be her boyfriend."

"Me? Why Me?"

"It's a wonder to me too. You sure are a little runt."

Fatty then opened her huge, bulbous mouth and sucked the bag of M&M's dry, then chewed the bag too (I assume for her daily fiber). She laughed with glee as she did this. She scooted closer to me as though to touch me. I stepped back to avoid her evil clutches only to fall over some bleachers and land on my backside. I looked up to see all three girls around me looking down. They were but shadows as the light of the moon and the stadium filled the space above me. Their horrible laughing pierced my ears. Fatty had another bag of M&M's in her hand, which she opened with her teeth, spitting out a small piece of the packaging. Her eyes were red in the darkness, and I was afraid. Very afraid.

So I would die a Virginian. I was pretty sure that's how the saying went. I wasn't sure what it meant. Out of nowhere a pair of hands flew from the night sky. One grasped heavily on Porky's wrist while the other wrestled away her bag of candy. A shadow appeared between me and the coven, eclipsing the stadium lighting so all I could see was his silhouette.

"We will let you know. Now run along."

"But that's my candy."

"No!" the silhouette yelled emphatically, "It's my candy now." Then he poured some of its contents into his mouth while the girls slunk back to their people.

It was F-ing Walsh. He had saved me.

Now we had a choice. Would I accept this offer or turn it down? Mike spoke first.

"I don't see a downside to this. She's pretty, she asked you, and we all know Katie is easy."

Dan spoke next, and when Dan spoke we always gave him great reverence. He only speaks when he has great wisdom to impart. "Yeah," he said.

"Plus that one girl has candy," added Walsh.

"Yeah, and she will have friends for us," Mike said.

"So it's settled, I will accept?"

"Yes, yes you will – for all of us."

"But," I asked, "who will go and tell them?"

I saw nothing but blank fear on the faces of my friends.

I couldn't be expected to go. That would be suicide. What if I had to talk to my new girlfriend? It was decided that Mike and Andrew would go and speak on my behalf and accept. F-ing Walsh would go along to search for more candy.

As the first quarter drew to an end my three brave brothers approached the huddled mass that was the girls from the eighth grade class of All Saints. They were big, and they were mean, but my three friends seemed undaunted in their approach. I couldn't hear what was said, but I saw some head nodding between the two groups. With the business side of things settled, the circle opened slightly and Katie appeared.

She appeared like the bloom of a flower from opening petals. It was my first look that night at my sudden new love. She was tall for her age, which would be an issue as I was short for any age. Her auburn hair was pulled back, with a slight curl forming at the end of the long strands. Her eyes darted from my ambassadors to me and back again. For my part, I slunk awkwardly behind Dan trying to look casual and not get caught staring at her. She caught my stare and locked in on me. A smile slowly played across her lips, and she let go of my eyes and looked shyly down at the ground. She dropped her eyelids, batting her lashes. She raised her eyes back to my gaze and replayed that smile. I, meanwhile, wet myself in fear. I think it may have gotten on Dan because he moved abruptly leaving me without any guard at all. I was in the open, completely unguarded.

Katie wore faded blue jeans and had wrapped herself in a heavy hoodie sweatshirt. She was, and still is, a beauty. When she laughed, she threw her head back and swished her hair back and forth. When she was nervous she would tug at the end of her hair and bite her lower lip. It was mesmerizing.

My men crossed back across the large chasm between us; the coven of girls watching them, scowls across their faces. Katie, however, had that lower lip under her front teeth and locked her stare on me. I returned the gaze, determined to not let her sense my fear.

When the men returned from their journey Mike spoke first.

"Done deal. I think you should grab her ass."

Walsh added, "They didn't have any more candy. All they had was some orange Tic-Tacs. Sorry."

By the beginning of the second quarter, Prep led North Central 7 to 0 and I had a girlfriend. The night was young and full of promise, but I couldn't help but think of a praying mantis that after coitus with her mate would kill him by ripping his head off. Somehow, I felt like I was in for the same fate.

As the second quarter passed the 8-minute mark, I noticed that my relationship with Katie had started to get stale. We were in the same boring pattern: I would look over at her and she would look away; I would keep staring, she would get uncomfortable and eventually leave; I would keep staring, but now at Carissa instead. Something needed to change before we lost sight of what brought us together in the first place. It was once again Mike who came up with an idea.

"You should tell her to meet you behind the bleachers."

"Then what?"

"Then you know, make out with her?"

"Don't you think it's too soon?" I asked

"Too soon? No. Remember, your goal is to at least grab her ass, maybe more."

"More what, like her thigh?"

"Higher," said Dan.

"I don't know that I can do this guys. How do we know if she is even into that?"

"What are you talking about, of course she's into it, " Mike proclaimed. "She's an All Saints girl, a Catholic schoolgirl. Everyone knows she'll be insulted if you don't try to make out with her."

Thus, it was decided. Katie and I would meet behind the bleachers at half time. No one in our time had ever attempted this. To convince a girl to leave the herd, let you grope her, and to do it within earshot of your peers and – even worse, parents – was an unthinkable risk. The only real flaw in the plan was that we had to get Katie to agree.

My delegation would handle everything. With three minutes left in the quarter Mike, Andrew, and Walsh walked solemnly across the chasm between our two groups and waited for Katie's representatives to arrive in the neutral middle ground. When both arrived, a very spirited conversation ensued.

Fatty was waiving her arms and pointing at Mike as he calmly nodded and pointed at the space behind the bleachers. She became more agitated and her arms flailed at great speed. Her eyes started to bug out and her face turned red. I am not sure if she inhaled for a full two minutes or not. I was tempted to end it all. Clearly, this was not what Katie had in mind for our relationship. We would be one of those couples who did not have sexual activity, like my parents. I tried to pull away and squash the whole negotiation, but I couldn't slip from Dan's grasp on my neck. I stared into the abyss and found Katie standing high on a bleacher looking my way. Not only did she seem intrigued by the summit, but she was watching my reaction. She even appeared, well, maybe excited by the thought of it.

When the men returned, it was with great satisfaction. Not only would we be meeting, but we also had to fulfill a seven-minute period alone together. If either one of us left early or chickened out there would be repercussions. If Katie left, Mike would be allowed to touch Carissa's leg from the knee to upper middle thigh. If I left early, Mike would never be allowed to talk to the girls again.

The game clock seemed bigger than life as it wound down. My stomach felt like I had swallowed fifteen pounds of buckshot. My legs were heavy and my heart was beating out of my chest.

This was the big time. I wasn't ready for the big time.

Dan had claimed to have experienced the big time with a public school girl. Her name was Molly and she would hang around after football practice to watch Dan. I had seen them kiss, but no tongue. He claimed they would sneak off to his basement, but there were no witnesses. Speaking of witnesses, Mike said we would need some to make sure I didn't chicken out. Andrew led a recon team under the bleachers to try finding an advisable vantage point to witness the debacle.

When the clock ran out and the end of the half sounded, I was green. I felt nauseous. I looked over at Katie and threw up a little in my mouth. This was awful. As the band took the field behind me I walked with Mike, Dan and Walsh to a quiet dark spot behind the north side of the bleachers. To the right was the bathroom and concession stand. We were tucked behind it. Katie was surrounded by her friends, but as soon as we showed our faces they started to disappear into the night. Mike tried to pull me together.

"Come on numb nuts, you can do this," he began. "She's ready for you; just go over there and get her. Don't let me down."

No words would escape my mouth. All I could do was nod. My mouth was dry. And then we were alone. We inched closer until she suddenly reached out and took my hand. I may have passed out.

The moment was electric. Over my right shoulder I could hear the guys trying to get a proper vantage point of our ordeal. I felt bad that they were spying on us until I saw Katie's coven over her left shoulder watching from the shadows. The fat one had a bag of pork rinds and anchored the trinity as the other two squirmed around her shoulders to see.

Katie leaned into my body, slowly sliding her hand from my palm up my arm and resting softly on my shoulder. She lifted her other hand gently onto my other shoulder. She slowly, nervously raised her eyes to meet mine. Even in the dark of the fall night I could see the power in her gaze. I was lost. On instinct my hands reached to her small waist and found the perfect resting place above her hips. The crowd around us created a white noise and I could hear the crunching as Fatty pounded down those pork rinds like it was her last meal.

I focused on Katie's eyes and everything else slowly faded into the dark of night. It was just Katie and I. We had this moment, forever. As I felt her soft form under the fabric of her sweatshirt it occurred to me that this moment was ours. Life would go on and it was likely that we would not spend it together. She would seek out happiness in the arms of another man; I would fall in love with another girl, but this moment belonged to the two of us. Our first real kiss. A first kiss holds such power for a young man and woman. You only get one. So I'd better not screw this up.

We were still arm's length apart and I could feel her hot breath. She took her hand and placed it on my heart and felt it racing. She giggled and took my hand off her waist and into her own and placed it over her heart so I could feel the rapid pace of our beating hearts and the warmth of her hand over mine. It was cold outside and yet my body was wet with perspiration. She took my hand and placed it on her cheek as she moved in closer to me. I could feel her body lean into mine and I was able make out her curves. I took my hand and swept her hair off her cheek and tucked it behind her ear.

Then our lips met.

At first it was a little awkward as our lips found their bearings, but then they just worked. She leaned into me until I felt like we were one. Her lips parted and then there was a tongue. It darted awkwardly from her mouth to mine. Not to be outdone, I took my tongue and ambushed her mouth with it, more assaulting than kissing. Then it was over. Our lips separated but I wouldn't let go of her waist.

"Should we do it again?" I asked, too afraid to hear the answer.

"Well, we do have six and a half minutes."

Back to work I went. This time I was determined to slide my hands from her waist to a lower position as instructed by Mike. I did this without any real argument from Katie. Maybe she just couldn't talk with her mouth full. After what seemed like an eternity, or at least six and a half minutes, we pulled ourselves apart.

"I like you," Katie said. "I hope you're my boyfriend for a long time."

"Really, why?"

She giggled. "There is something about you. You make me feel safe."

"Walsh beat me up. Is that going to be a problem?"

"No."

"Okay. I just thought you should know."

"Okay."

Our magical halftime had come to an end, and the game started again. We walked back to our bleacher seats with her hand entwined in mine. When we came to the chasm between our respective groups she turned to me and looked me square in the eye, smiled, and pulled away. It occurred to me suddenly that I had forgotten something important and I pulled her hand back into mine.

"Oh, shit. I was supposed to grab your boobs."

She smiled and pulled her hand back. She was gone. We watched her walk back to her coven. I stood, jelly-legged and spent from what had just happened. Understandably, all the blood had rushed from my head and it was now trying to get back to its proper stations, making me weak. I knew something special had just happened. A rush of adrenaline .

overcame my body and I needed an outlet. My group of friends, patting me on the back, engulfed me.

"Did you do it?" Walsh asked. "Did you grab her ass?"
"Yeah, I did, and I put my tongue in her mouth." I raised my hands over my head like a heavyweight champion.

"And I think she is going to let me touch her boobs," I screamed to the stars above.

"They feel like warm water balloons," Mike added, as if he knew.

I was the Casanova of this group. I was going to touch her boobs. I sprinted up the bleacher steps out into the concourse with so much adrenaline pumping through my body that I had to run it off before I imploded. Then I was sprinting around the outside of the stadium. All the boys followed behind me, intrigued to learn more. After two laps Dan squared me up and tackled me to the ground and a dog pile ensued, but I wouldn't tell more. Besides no matter how often they asked or how often I told them I could never do the moment justice. It can only be understood by those who have been there, by those who have felt each other's heart race with fear and anticipation.

Katie and I will share that moment for a lifetime.

Third Quarter

When we returned to our rightful place amongst the riff-raff at the 20-yard line, Prep had built a dominant lead. Up 21-0, it looked like they might run away with the game. I sat on a bench pondering what had just happened. When I was getting ready for the game, my goal for the night was not to be thrown into the dumpster again like I had the weekend before by some freshmen. It never occurred to me that something like this might happen, that by the third quarter of the game I would be in a loving relationship with a beautiful girl whom I had always assumed was out of my league.

Yet here I was, content and in love, with the memory of her tongue jabbing frantically at my back molars fresh in my mind. On top of that, I felt like I was finally a part of a group in a way that I hadn't been before. The way my friends looked at me now that I had grabbed Katie's butt was different. I could see the respect in their eyes. I had gone where no man had gone before – certainly none of the novices circling around me now.

I was so happy as I sat there on that bench. Were all my dreams really going to come true? I looked casually over at Katie. She stood rigid and straight, looking over the mass of bodies to the game on the field below. Her back arched, pushing her hips back and creating a curve. As an eighth grader, I was really starting to notice these things. Her scarf hung awkwardly, exposing some of her neck to the elements and my eyes. She caught me staring at her and smiled at me. I shamefully smiled back and then bore my eyes into the cement beneath my feet. I was wearing big clunky snow boots that my mother had insisted I wear. There was no snow, of course, but that didn't matter since her goal was to mock me in front of my friends and to ensure I died a virgin. I didn't need her help dying a virgin, I could do it myself. But now things were looking up.

"What do we do now?" I asked Mike

"Not sure, does she have any friends for us?"

"You saw them."

"Ugh, no thanks," commented Dan from the back.

"I am okay with them," started Mike. "They aren't quality, but they're here."

"Well what do we do?"

"We have to come up with some sort of plan to get them to come over and talk to us. It has to be organic though, it can't feel forced," Mike suggested.

Walsh added, "What if we just slowly move our group over closer to them? We can just start talking to them when we are standing next to them. It will seem natural, and if we go slow enough it will seem like we have been there the whole time."

It was both brilliant and foolproof. We gathered the circle in tight and put our arms around each other. We slowly moved across the chasm. Our feet churned over benches and steps. Andrew periodically poked his head out in order to steer.

"Two clicks west." Pound pound pound.

"Okay one click east by northeast."

"What is a click?"

"Who cares? Anyone know where northeast is?"

"Is that a star? I am just saying maybe we can use the stars as a compass."

"Just turn left, dumbass."

Pound pound pound.

It felt like a million years by the time we had zig-zagged through the gulf between our two groups, yet only a minute and eleven seconds had bled off the game clock.

Of course, the girls had noticed our approach, and they glared at us. Things softened, however, when Katie came across our circle, opening both groups in her wake, and threw her arms around me in an embrace. She dropped the hug, and then muscled Andrew half a click northwest to make room for herself. She clung tightly to my hand.

Then we were one: girls next to boys, laughter and smiles, banter. It had worked by God; it had worked. It was then that an adult moment washed over me. I was getting these more and more often as I sped towards being a grown-up myself. This may be the best of it, I thought. The joy and wonder I felt now may be eternal. I knew I would never forget Katie, but I also couldn't expect her to be in love with me forever. I knew deep down that this moment was a gift.

She could change her mind on a whim. Women do that, you know. I could picture her in her white wedding gown, her smile radiating, eyes brimming with tears of joy. I pictured such beauty as she walked down the aisle. What I couldn't picture was myself next to her. She deserved so much better, someone taller, someone who had defined muscles, someone like Joe Gaukroger. I squeezed Katie's hand tighter at the thought of him coming near her. She smiled at my show of affection and then pulled her hand from mine in pain.

Joe was the source of many of our fears. We ran into him from time to time. He was a public-school kid, hulking in a brutish, sullen sort of way. Not even the high school kids messed with him. Stronger than everyone else, he was the desire of many girls. Most of us avoided places he could be on the off chance he decided you would become his next target. He wasn't above mocking you to tears in front of people. If you did decide to fight back, he would wrap you into a pretzel and toss you to the side. Rumor had it he had flunked seventh grade three times and could already drive. He certainly looked old enough. He often bought beer for all of his friends, and he never recycled the cans. As well as being a bully and stealing our girls, he consistently raped mother earth. Whatever Joe wanted, he tended to get it.

I didn't have to worry about that right now. I was with Katie in this moment. Where we would go or what the future held was just that – the future. In this moment a beautiful girl was holding my hand and resting her head on my scrawny shoulder.
When the whistle blew and the third quarter came to an end, Prep led North Central by 34 points. All seemed right in the world.

Then all the hair on my neck stood up as I sensed a shift in the wind.

I saw him as a shadow at first. If he hadn't moved I would have assumed he was just a stupid, inarticulate tree. Then he moved. Slowly, with his knuckles dragging on the cement and his back hunched, he strode towards us. We were spotted. Children and cats scattered in his wake, terrified. A dog barked only to have the hulking form grab the dog and strangle it, or at least he certainly could have.

Smiling, Joe Gaukroger approached us. He shoved me to the ground and stepped on my chest and placed his freakishly well-muscled arm around Katie. He smiled with glee and said, "Hey guys."

Oh shit. Joe Gaukroger was here, and he wanted my girlfriend. I had a bad feeling about this, and it wasn't just his boot squeezing all the air out of my lungs.

And thus started the fourth quarter.

Fourth Quarter

Joe Gaukroger was handsome in the way a baby born with large tumors about his head is handsome. He was a mystery that your human eyes would never see live again; you would have had no choice but to stare at him. Sometimes I couldn't believe he wasn't just some horrible nightmare induced by the extra Ritalin pills my mother would stuff down my throat when she wanted me to do her bidding. I had been taking Ritalin for the last several months, ever since my mother found me pounding my forehead on my bedroom wall in frustration. She thought it was a psychiatric fit, but it was in fact born of an encounter with Megan where we had tangled our braces together while kissing and had to be removed by Laura and Mike pulling at our waists in different directions. I can still hear the screams of pain and weeping tears. I think Megan was hurt, too.

Anyhow, Joe had now enveloped my beautiful girlfriend in his big meaty stupid hand. I may have been wrong but I thought I saw her try to pull away only to have Joe's paw dig deeper into the soft part of her shoulder. Joe's eyes darted from girl to girl, sizing up his prey. Joe wanted them all. Not a word was spoken as Joe sucked the air out of the circle. It was Ursula, the fat one, that spoke first. What did she have to worry about? She was the one girl there that Joe had no interest in.

"So Joe, what brings you here?"

"My bike, I rode my bike," he responded in several guttural grunts.

"Yes Joe. I meant, why are you here?" Ursula prodded softly.

49

I had never realized before how meek Ursula's voice was. I was always distracted by the fact that she never seemed to talk without stuffing her face full of potato chips, chocolate, and corn dogs.

"I heard Katie was going to the game and I figured she would want to see me," Joe rumbled.

With that, he gave that beautiful and soft ivory shoulder a rough squeeze. Katie's eyes pleaded into mine; she seemed to beg for help. My skin had gone ashen. The muscles of my body were too weak to move; even the muscles of my throat seemed unable to swallow gulps of air. I knew I needed to do something, but what?

My mind raced with scenarios but every one of them ended with me picking up my teeth and placing them in a Ziploc bag. Joe turned towards the field of action, pulling Katie's shoulder, and thus the rest of her, away from me. She turned her head back to me and feebly raised her hand out to mine imploring my help. My fingers trembled and it took all my strength to stretch my arm out to her. But Joe had pulled her out of my reach.

"What do I do, what do I do?" I thought. How was this possible? Mere moments ago I'd had it all. My sweaty palm had been embracing hers. I could still smell the essences of her perfume in the air around me. She was so close, and yet so far. I was frozen in fear.

Chris Kordash had once stood up to Joe, and no one had seen him since. Theories abounded that he was dead, or at least so disfigured he and his family had to go into hiding.

I could always count on Mike to come to my aid and put things into perspective.

"What are you, some sort of pussy?" Mike challenged.

"Yeah, I think I might be," I responded. "It would certainly explain why I'm numb."

"Do you or do you not love Katie?" he asked.

"Of course I do. Everything I do, I do it for her." Bryan Adams is a poet.

"Then fight for her. Win her love."

"I thought I had when she had her tongue in my mouth."

"That's not love. You don't have love until at least third base."

I had to admit Mike had a point there.

"Mike, what I am supposed to do, fight him? He has the DNA of a demented gorilla."

"Yes, you fight him. You stand like a man and you fight for what is rightfully yours. Just last quarter, mere moments ago, you had her resting her head on your shoulder; you had her hand in yours. She was yours man. Now someone wants to take that from you. Well I say 'no.' We stand here. We draw the line. No matter how big or how strong a man is he cannot defeat the true heart and soul of a good man. You're not alone in this fight; we are standing right beside you. Not even Joe can defeat a group of true friends."

A wave of adrenaline washed over me. What did I have to fear? I was a man made of flesh and blood just like him. Well, sort of. My flesh was saggy and unformed and my blood currently ran cold, but still, the basic cellular principle was the same. Besides I had an army of good men beside me, my friends. Katie was mine. I would fight for her. I would win her. Love would prevail.

Yet a nervous and doubting voice in my head kept asking, "But what if he kills you? What if you literally die?"

No. That was not going to happen. Fate would not allow it, and if it did, I would have died a man fighting for love. Is there anything more noble?

To be honest and historically accurate, it wasn't a voice in my head, but Andrew standing behind me urgently whispering it over and over in my ear.

The two-minute warning sounded in the game. A warning, but to whom? To me, to Joe? This was going to be resolved here, tonight. By the time that clock struck zero I would hold my love in my arms or I would die for her.

I slowly approached the chasm Joe and Katie now filled, their backs to me. My brothers in arms fell in behind. I hadn't noticed them slowly backing up.

"Joe," I said. It was really more of a squeak, and no one could hear it. I would have to do it again. I steeled all my resolve and tried again.

"Joe, I'm talking to you."

Joe turned leisurely to face me. He looked over me as I only came up to his navel.

He turned back towards the field assuming it was the wind that had carried his name. I wanted to tap him on the shoulder but I lacked the vertical athletic ability to do so. Instead I tickled him on the kidney. He giggled and turned and looked down on me.

"What is it little man?" he asked.

"I am not that little. And, and…that's my girl. Katie is my girl, you hear me?"

"Oh my God, he's adorable." With that Joe rustled my hair with his paw and turned back to the game. Katie looked at me pleadingly. At least I think it was pleading. In retrospect, it could have been gas or maybe pity.

I pulled every fiber of strength and focused it on the fist I had made with my right hand. I reared back and punched Joe in the lower back with all my might. Joe didn't notice. I panicked. Not knowing what to do next I fell to my knees and bit his calf. My braces dug into his skin, leaving small punctures. Joe screamed and kicked me off his leg. I scrambled to my feet. I didn't know what to do next. My eyes darted from the intense redness of Joes face to the look of helpless concern on Katie's. At least I knew I had my brothers behind me, a force to reckon with. I turned to reassure myself and the little turncoats were scurrying up the stairs in fear. I was on my own, a dead man walking.

Joe raised his fist towards the sky. It all happened so slowly. My eyes found Katie's and darted to the game clock. Five seconds left. The fist reached its apex and began its descent towards my face. Four seconds. My eyes widened in fear. Three seconds. A large moon served as a backdrop in a starless sky as his fist hurtled towards the bridge of my nose. Two seconds. My life raced before me. It hadn't been much, but it quickly played out in my mind. The fights with my little brother, the Christmas dinners with my mother and father singing around a piano, the hugs before bed and the prayers as we turned out the lights. Wait a minute, that's not my life. I was watching someone else's life, a better life, before I died. That just figures. One second. I raised my hands in front of my face to try to ward off the attack. Zero. The horn blew. It was all over.

His fist broke easily through my hands and landed flush with the bridge of my nose. The blow staggered me backwards towards the metal bleachers. I refused to go down so easily and I reached for anything to steady my beleaguered body. My hand rested on a bleacher seat but only for a moment as the second blow found its mark on my cheekbone and drove me towards the ground. I could taste the blood coming from my broken nose. I fell to the ground and rolled over to see the heavens. I would be there shortly, I thought. Perhaps my beloved dog Scorpio would greet me. My eyeballs danced, trying to focus. Moments before I blacked out a beautiful face came into my gaze. It was Katie. I saw the concern on her face. Her eyes shimmered with life. Her skin glittered in the moonlight. Never before had she had looked so beautiful. Her skin was so clear and soft. As she leaned forward I could once again smell her sweet scent. I could still feel her lips pressed to mine.

This life, this death, had all been for the one moment of her kiss. Though I now knew I would die, I would die a man, a man who'd had the love of a good woman – a woman who had let him get to second base and likely third, had halftime been longer. The fourth quarter was over, but I had known love. Is that not a victory for any man? In our life can we ask for more? I say not. It was becoming fuzzy as my mind started to shut down, but I could see sweet Katie's face.

"I think we should just be friends," she said.

And then I died.

The Dance

The life of a young teen is filled with climactic moments, moments that will be repeated often later in life but never with the same crackle and spark as they did back when everything meant nothing, but nothing meant everything. We think of first kisses, the first time we held hands, maybe the first time we take a smoke or have a drink.

For me, a real landmark in my young life was my first dance. We had all practiced what it would be like to touch a girl. Dan had filled a couple of water balloons with warm fluid to about half full to approximate the experience.

"That," he said, "is about what it feels like to touch a girl's breast."

Dan was three months older than the rest of us and had been seen hanging out with a public school girl, (who we all knew were sluts). Taking the mystery out of boobs would be a huge advantage at a dance. This would allow us to not be surprised, bewildered, nor in such shock that we passed out if we accidentally grazed a breast while dancing, which we all hoped would happen.

Junior high school dances are not unlike the culling of a herd. The haves and have-nots were separated into groups to be judged by the girls that huddled on the opposite side of the gym. The fate of each was decided well before the dance started, but hope springs eternal. No matter who it was, each young lad felt that there might be a chance for survival; the fact is, there was likely none. Like ethnic cleansing, most were doomed by simply being born into a certain DNA class. They had no control over who they were or what they looked like; they were simply born that way. Yet the ruling class (always women) called the shots. If you were out, you were socially dead, a useless sack of skin and bones. A man would call on any advantage to survive. If that advantage was that he knew his way around a warm water balloon breast, so be it.

It was a cool, damp December Friday night when the seventh and eighth graders of All Saints met in the small, slightly musty gym to watch what was akin to a slaughter. Of course, proper manners decry we call it a dance, but it was a slaughter. Boys lined up against walls shoulder to shoulder while girls mowed them down with their rejecting eyes. This dance would have been no different except I had a plan.

The goal was always the same: to get Katie, Megan, or Laura to fall in love with me. It didn't matter whom; in fact, I had a rule that it was first come, first served. In order to do this I would need to stand out from the crowd. I figured that if I appeared tough enough I would be in. I had watched a Michael Jackson video that very afternoon (before he started touching little boys in their no-no places). Not only did he have some moves where his legs fluttered about and he twisted around at all angles, but he did so in a white t-shirt with rolled up sleeves and a cigarette behind his ear. I owned a white t-shirt with only minor pit stains, and I still had a pack of my grandma's Virginia Slims. I would need to pin up my sleeves because I didn't have the biceps to hold them up, but that seemed a simple fix.

My mother dropped me off outside the gym. She had dressed me in corduroy slacks and a mustard yellow shirt with a brown clip-on tie. I angled in the shadows of the building, being careful not to be seen, and found a spot behind the dumpsters to pull off the shirt and tie and roll my sleeves up. I would have to live with the corduroy pants. Hopefully no one would see my pants anyhow – unless someone got into them…oh yeah. Of course I can make those jokes because these things just never really happened. As I used paper clips to hold up the rolled sleeves of my white t-shirt, I realized I had failed to complete the look. I forgot the cigarette that pulled the whole badass look together. I scrambled inside to find Dan.

"Dan, Dan I need your help! I need to borrow your bike."

"My bike? No way man."

"Come on; I have to or there is no way I'll score. I left something really important at home."

"Like what?"

"Like the finishing touches to my ensemble. My badass ensemble, the type that drives the women crazy."

"There is not an outfit in the world that would help you with women."

"Come on man, you got your public-school girl; you touch her boobs all the time. I have nothing. I have a package of balloons and a dream. I thought you were my friend."

"Jesus, fine. Just go. Anything is better than this whining. Just don't wreck it."

Dan treasured his yellow ten-speed. Dan's family was modest in wealth and didn't flaunt a lot of money. Clothes were hand-me-downs, but this bike was all Dan's. He had saved for months on his paper route to purchase the perfect bike.

As I rode Dan's perfect bike to my house to sneak in the backyard and find the cigarette under the flowerpot by the back shed, I began to reflect on my hopes for the evening. I wasn't sure at the time which girl I would try to charm first.

My instinct told me to just hang back and see how it played out, but that sounded silly. The right thing to do was to suffocate all three girls with my presence until one of them gave in and danced with me, thereby sparing the other two my annoying existence.

After easily locating the cigarette and tucking it in my pocket, I started the trek back to the gym. The return trip was mostly downhill. In fact, when I arrived on the final leg of the journey I shot down a hill to the gym as if out of a cannon. In winter the locals like to sled on this slope as it has a sharp drop that panned out at the bottom. If you wanted to get to the gym you needed to take a sharp right three-quarters of the way down. As I started to speed down the hill, the wind whipping at my face, a memory surfaced.

Since two Saturdays ago when he snapped the hand brakes off, Dan had to plan his stops in advance. That meant he had no brakes. Since I was going at a fast clip, this worried me. Nevertheless, my panicked mind surfaced with a plan – if I took a sharp right into the gym parking lot I could hit a fence post, smash the front wheel of the bike into the pole and then stop by using my face as a brake. That sounded like a serviceable concept, so that's what I did. As I slid the twenty-five feet that the force of the abrupt collision had imparted on my body, I started to reflect on the plan as a possible mistake. I could feel the asphalt collect under the skin of my face and then I was pretty sure I should have just ridden down to the bottom of the hill and stopped using gravity like Dan did.

When I came to a halt, I felt a sharp pain in my knee. I was surprised to find that my kneecap had curled to the side of my leg. It looked unnatural and may have made it difficult to do my Michael Jackson black-guy dance (this was when Michael Jackson was still black). What was worse was that the cigarette was now in five pieces. I took the butt and put it behind my ear, but with the blood and scabbing of my face I felt that I wouldn't look nearly as tough as I had hoped. I picked up the front wheel of Dan's bike, which had conveniently rolled the twenty-five feet away from the accident, and walked towards the gym. The front wheel was more rhombus-shaped then circular, and Dan was shocked when I placed it in has arms.

"Sorry. Your brakes are a little sticky."

"I hope you broke your fucking leg."

"I'm pretty sure I did. Okay, where are the women at?" I asked, scanning the room.

The atmosphere at the dance was as I expected – stale and with a waft of terror in the air. The boys hung in small tight circles around the outside of the east wall of the gym. On the west wall the girls spread about, stalking their prey in small figure-eight paths, their eyes darting from boy to boy. Sometimes their rhythmic paths would be disrupted by one girl grabbing the arms of another and flooding the middle of the floor with a spastic muscle jerk that I guess was dancing but appeared more like a severe seizure to me.

I sauntered up to Laura and ran my fingers through my hair, greasing it back. In the process I took my cigarette from behind my right ear. It fell out, which led to me leaning over and picking it off my shoe. As I bent over Dan was kind enough to notice that in the tragic bike crash I had split the seat of my pants. The girls giggled, but I assumed it was because they had noticed the extra work I had been doing on the muscles of my buttocks.

When I got a hold of the beat I started to dance – not just dance, but Dance (with a capital "D"). I took my right leg and wrapped it around my left leg and spun. I did this with my arms raised to the side. I then took two moonwalk steps back and repeated the gesture. I then took my right leg and quickly stepped over my left and then my left over my right and repeated often. I took my arms and pumped them as if running, but it was really just to help me keep my balance.

"What are you doing?" asked Dan.

"Isn't it obvious?" Laura giggled. "He is having a stroke."

"Is that true?" asked Walsh while eating an entire slice of pizza in one bite.

"No. I'm dancing."

"That's not dancing," said Mike.

"Yes, it is. That's how black guys dance. I saw it on TV."

"Black guys don't dance like that."

"Yes, they do. Ask Matt."

Matt was the only black guy we knew. In a strange bit of irony, he was also the only guy any of us had met who took ballet. We assumed that made him not only the only black guy we knew but also the only gay guy we knew. He would later have sex with Andrew's sister and then rob our house, so I guess that just shows that you cannot stereotype people. There is no way I would have guessed he would have slept with Andrew's sister. Her ass is normal sized.

Matt immediately dismissed the claims that black people danced that way and to prove his point he gracefully lifted one leg over his head and spun in a dazzling fashion away from us.

Panic was on the fringes of my psyche. If my black-guy dance was not going to charm the ladies, I was done. I didn't have another bullet for the gun. Dejected, I decided to pull myself out of the line of fire and try to regroup. The new objective was to slow dance with a girl in the hope that maybe she would accidentally allow me to kiss her. In that kiss I would try to insert my tongue into her mouth. Now, I knew the risks about bacteria in a girl's mouth, and that a girl's tongue was the most unsanitary object in the world, but I was willing to take that risk. If I was able to slip her the tongue, as the kids are calling it today, I was going to try to lower my hands from her lower back to her butt – grazing at first, but if I didn't sense an objection I intended to get a full handful. Mike wrote out all these instructions for me ahead of time on the back of my hand. He didn't want me to screw this up.

I went to the bathroom to examine myself and prepare for battle. It wasn't good. I had a dark, brooding knot growing on my forehead. A road rash extended from my cheek down my arm and side. I had to pick small pebbles from the wound with my fingernails. A yellow hue was taking hold under my eye.

I splashed my face with cool water and prepped myself to return to the battlefield. I could do this. I just needed to wait for the right slow song and ask the closest girl to dance. Hopefully fate would shine down on me and the closest girl would be both attractive and desperate for attention.

Bodies milled about on the gym floor, not so much dancing as flailing in and out of the rhythm of the music. I settled in a corner where I was in striking distance of the girls, but far enough away to not be seen as an immediate threat. Then it happened. Bad English rang through the speakers, the perfect slow song. And then a girl came into my view – tall for her age, with straight blond hair and heavy green eyes. She had any easy smile to her that flashed gently to all who saw it.

Laura. I had played plenty of spin the bottle with her, but she didn't have a choice in those games. Now I was planning on asking her to dance to a slow song, with my hands on her body. I needed to act fast. These songs are not long, three minutes tops. That feels like an eternity when you're dancing, but in reality, it's a short time to try to dance, kiss, slip tongue, slide your hands to lower back then to ass. I approached quickly, taking a sidewinder path so as to hide my mangled face.

"Laura I was thinking we could...."

"Sure," she said thrusting herself towards me quickly.

Her arms landed on my shoulders and her elbows locked so that I was forced to be an arm's length away. This was an issue because Laura had longer arms than I did. This left me flailing about trying to reach anything on Laura and left me grabbing at air. Laura sighed and unlocked her elbows, allowing me to hold her closer than she or anyone related to her desired me to. Not knowing where to put my arms, I put them on her shoulders to match the pair she had on mine. Not only was this awkward looking as we tottered side to side but it was also uncomfortable as our elbows kept bumping into each other.

"You're supposed to put your arms on my waist," she said.

"Really, you will let me do that?"

"Yes, it's called dancing."

"I am not sure what it's called but I think it's wonderful."

I slid my hands to rest just above her hips. I could feel the warmth of her skin under the fabric of her shirt. I could feel her hips sway side to side. As Bad English continued explaining how great it was to see someone smile, I thought about the next step in my plan: the kiss.

I pulled Laura casually towards me until I could feel her chest on mine. She was taller than I so I had to look up into her eyes. They were not as cross-eyed as I had originally thought. I slowly tried to lean in, giving her the hint that this was the kissing moment. For a heartbeat it was as if no one else was in the gym. It was just Laura and I with a private show by Bad English. As I leaned ever closer Laura stood her ground; her fingers dug into my shoulders. Then a giggle from the crowd, followed by laughter, followed by a gasp, and finally exclamations of "oh my god that is so gross."

The moment passed. Laura was so shamed by the others that she quickly retreated to the bathroom with her friends. Of course I was left standing alone on the floor. The lights were dim but concealed little. With no Laura to block me, my joy of the moment was evident in my corduroys. There was no concealing this with schoolbooks at the end of class. I turned quickly and headed to the corner with my back to the crowd. The girls that had not left with Laura to the bathroom raced on to pass the word of the flag-raising that had happened in their absence.

There would be no dancing, no kiss, no tongue – just shame and future therapy visits. I had been cut down like the others, yet another victim of this genocide. As I left the gym I bowed my head and focused my eyes on the tips of my shoes. I wanted to look no man in the eye; I just wanted to die in peace.

As I entered the hallway I missed the gaggle of girls exiting the bathroom. I ran right back into Laura. Disgusted now, she grunted and moved briskly away from my wretched sight. In our collision I had inadvertently felt her left boob. It was nothing like a warm water balloon. Nevertheless, it made the night a success. I walked home content and fulfilled and quickly fell asleep. There it was at last. Third base. We must be in love.

Keefe Bowl

Pat Keefe was a skinny kid with sharp facial features and a quiet calm about him. More importantly, his backyard was the size of a pasture. This meant we could play football in it. At thirteen years of age, the acreage seemed as immense as Soldier Field to me. The yard was lined with juniper bushes on one side and rose bushes on the other, making an enjoyable treat for anyone that went out of bounds in a standard game of tackle football. This was Pat Keefe's yard and the home of The Keefe Bowl.

Playing football was new to me at this point in my life. Not being one to try new things that may require pain, I had shied away from the contact that was required by sports such as football, wrestling, and a strange playground game that Mike had introduced called bloody knuckles. I guess the object of bloody knuckles was to break your opponent's hand by punching their knuckles with your own. This was not one of Mike's best ideas but still better than his bloody testicles game, in which you kick each other in the groin until one of your testicles climbs back up into your body cavity for protection.

Dan had the idea to play a football game. There had been some tension around school. At a small private Catholic school, there were bound to be those families that were born into money. The families with large homes and ski condos abounded. I was one of them. Make fun of me all you want but my 86-degree heated pool was delightful in the evening. On the other side of the ledger were those people who couldn't even afford a ledger. Those were the big Catholic families that were sending children to the school on scholarship. Those were the parents that attended Sunday mass every week and always had the kids in tow. They didn't have two nickels to rub together, but they did all the work that the school needed. Those were the classroom moms that prepared all the art projects and field trips. Those were the dads who coached the school basketball team and ran the school carnival.

I seemed to always fall in tow with the poor kids more than the rich ones. To be honest, neither of them really liked me, but the poor kids were more Christian about it. Even at a tender age those that had less resented those that had much. The lucky guys with the extra toys never seemed to understand why the others didn't enjoy their show and tell as much as they did. Some kids played with a stick and it was a hand me down.

Dan presented the idea at recess one day after we had played a game of touch football on the cement.

"We need to take this up a notch," he said. "We need to punish each other with some tackle football."

As he finished the sentence he clothes-lined a sixth-grader who had had the audacity to run through our game. It was okay; the kid regained consciousness before school let out.

"I just feel like I need to hit something," Dan concluded.

We all agreed. Bloody testicles was a nice activity, but we needed a man's sport.

As the afternoon rolled on, in Sister Mary Ann's class we started to draft up teams. Dan was the first pick as he was by far the best athlete in the school. F-ing Walsh was taken and then Mike, and so on, until there was a team. I went undrafted but was asked to join late because I promised to bring Gatorade.

As the list of teams was passed around one couldn't help but notice the economic divide between them. Brian Sweeney, Pat Keefe, and Cody Coombs, who all came from the nice area of town, sat on one side while those that lived below 29th Street balanced out the other.

Later, when we were in high school, the game would be played weekly on Sunday mornings throughout the winter. In adulthood, the game would commence on the day after Christmas. During all that time the teams changed very little. Pictures from those later games would dot the offices of those involved. It was a great game with great friends, but the first match started with a message: We have a lot of anger and we don't know how else to control it other than hitting each other.

It was the early winter of my eighth-grade year when the first Keefe Bowl took place. I was thirteen and I had just lost my dad, at least for an extended amount of time. My father had been a functional alcoholic since he was eighteen. After a couple of tours in Vietnam he came back home, cracked a couple beers, got married, and had kids. He worked for his father-in-law running a chain in one of his lumber mills. Over time he would take over and manage the mill for the family. All the while he had his companion, Coors, with him. He was a hard worker with a quiet demeanor but had a sharp wit when needed. He did the work but over time he sank further and further into an abyss that seemed to feed his need for alcohol.

I never noticed an issue. Dad always seemed the same to me. He wasn't a fall down drunk or abusive or anything; he just was. However, the fights between my parents had grown more heated. Parents think that the kids are in tune with all the drama that the marriage presents them, but they really aren't. Kids don't care. You are the source for cable and food and an occasional ride to school-sanctioned events.

Everything else is your issue. In fact, the first time I even realized there was a problem was on a Tuesday night in the den. Dad and I had circled up on the couch. I was falling asleep on his shoulder because he had insisted on watching M*A*S* H.

M*A*S*H is every bit as effective as Ambien in putting people to sleep. When I looked up the man had his eyes filled with tears. It was the first time he had cried in front of me. I didn't think he was capable of it. When I asked what was wrong he shrugged it off.

"Just the show; it is tough for me to watch."

I took him at his word, but looking back it wasn't the show. It was a life changing decision he had made that caused his unrest. The next day he packed his meager belongings and left. He left a job that paid well; he left a house that was more then he could imagine with huge rooms, a pool, and a staff that did the cleaning and caretaking. He left a family with more money than they needed, and all his friends as well. He left and was alone. He left his kids. He left his drinking. He checked into a rehab for six weeks, and when it was all said and done his marriage was over.

For my part, all I knew was that he was gone for six weeks and his new place didn't have cable – just the 3 networks and PBS. I preferred bloody testicles to spending the weekend there.

When kickoff for Keefe Bowl started, six girls (including, Katie, Laura and Megan) stood on the sidelines along with one little sister. That was Mike's sister Krissy, who wasn't a real person anyhow so she didn't count.

And my Dad.

I hadn't seen him in those six weeks, but he looked the same to me. Later in life I would learn that he was truly risking his life if he kept drinking. He had considered drinking himself to death, but had chosen this instead: daily fear and doubt if he had the strength to stay away from the drink, a one bedroom apartment, a $12,000 a year job selling fertilizer in bulk to ranches and farms, and watching his son play football with his friends. It would be one of many games that he watched me play in, be it football, basketball, or baseball. He also made all the choir concerts and theater shows. He was always there because he chose to believe in his own resolve to beat his affliction and not quit on his kids, even when they quit on him or themselves. I am not sure everyone could give up a life with boats, jets, and club memberships (not to mention the sweet nurturing arms of booze) to live a pauper's life.

But he did. And on a Sunday morning at Keefe Bowl, there he was, for me.

As per the rules, the game would be tackle. You had four plays to get to the tree that marked the middle of the field and four plays from there to score. When you ran out of plays the ball would be turned over to the opponent. The junipers and rose bushes marked the perilous out of bounds. The start of the basketball court was one end zone and the stairs to the porch the other.

The poor kids from below 29th Street started with the ball. Dan was at his customary QB spot and quickly rolled out. With no one open and the defense bearing down, he pressed the line of scrimmage and made a cut to the inside and then a nifty spin move. Moving towards the opposite sideline he angled himself past one defender then cut back hard, watching another defender fly by him. He then scampered easily into the end zone. Dan was being his über-athletic self. The defense would need to put two people on him. They used my guy, as I was pretty worthless.

I excelled on defense. As it turned out, I was a pretty angry person. On the first play from scrimmage, Brian angled himself on a sweep toward the roses. He planned to cut back, but I was able to pin him in, and I wrapped him up and drove my feet until we both landed in the bushes. Blood bubbled up through small lacerations on my arms. Blood. It felt right.

The teams squared each other up. Dan led our assault while Pat controlled the balanced passing attack of the rich kids. At half time it was all even. Then the surreal happened. Appearing out of the trees that blocked off the lot from the street came one Joe Gaukroger. Big and brooding, he strode with purpose toward us. He wasn't going to play, was he? That wasn't fair; he was too big and athletic and he had a full beard. I think he had already served in the Navy. More importantly, he was a public school kid, which made him poor, which meant he should play for us.

"No way," said Pat Keefe "He lives on our side of 29th."

"No, he doesn't," answered Walsh "He lives 2 blocks from me on 12th."

"No, his parents live on 12th, Joe is under house arrest at his uncle's on 33rd. He has cable."

Shit. We would have to defend him.

"Wait," I said, trying to repay the loyalty the poor kids had provided by selecting me. "He can't play – the teams would be uneven."

"That's alright. You guys can have Mike's sister, Krissy."

70

"She's a girl," I pleaded.

"She's faster than you are."

That was true. She had already beaten me in a sprint across the yard. Shit. This was going from bad to worse.

As was expected, Joe dominated the game. He was impossible to bring down. At one point I tackled him by jumping on his back, pulling his wool hat over his eyes and punching him in both ears. If he hadn't tripped over a sprinkler head, I'm not sure it would have worked. Dan did his best to keep us in the game with some dazzling runs, but it was only a matter of time before we would succumb to our opponents.

The game was to go to seven by ones. With the score 6-4 Joe took off left and ran over both Mike and Andrew and slipped out of the grasp of Dan. I had an angle on him just before the goal line. All of my anger built as I ran and prepared to unload on him. Not just the fact that he stole Katie from me, or the fact that he had made fun of me over the course of the day, but also the anger about my parents' divorce all boiled up in my body, ready to explode. As the collision neared at the goal line I struck with my forearms, rising as I extended my hips through the tackle. My forearms found their mark under his chin and jolted him back. The collision sent both of us sprawling into the junipers. Joe was shocked by the impact – but only for a moment. I, however, was concussed and would be for three years.

"Touchdown," Joe said, raising his arms.

"Bullshit!" I responded. "You didn't get past the rose bushes on to the basketball court."

"The ball crossed the plane."

"No, it didn't. You're down."

Now Joe looked at me with red glaring eyes. His left eye twitched under the burden of his anger. He clenched his teeth and stood inches from my face.

"I said I scored."

With this he shoved me hard to the ground. I quickly jumped up but didn't know what to do. Joe's clenched fist marked my chest and he shoved me down again, this time with severe malice.

I got up and looked around the crowd. No one was going to step forward and defend my ruling. This was between Ugly and me.

"Tell me I scored," he said. "Tell me I scored and I won't kick your ass in front of all your friends and my girlfriend Katie over there."

My fist clinched and then released. I looked over to my Dad. He stood 50 yards away, watching, but content to let me fight my own fight. I was pissed because I knew he had a hunting rifle in the car. He would be of no help. I backed down.

"Fine, Joe, you scored."

A groan came from my teammates as this signaled the end of Keefe Bowl I. Joe excitedly proclaimed his victory and then took the football and left. It was Andrew's football. As the field cleared and people started to head home, my father came up to me and put his arm around my sulking shoulders.

"Good game," he said. "Hell of a tackle at the end."

"Why didn't you help me with Joe? You didn't do anything?"
"Like what?"

"I don't know – something you learned in the war."

"You had it under control. You know enough to fight the fights that need to be fought."

"I was afraid."

My eyes filled with tears as I said this.

"Is that why you're upset?"

"No. I'm upset because I let someone better me because I was afraid."

"Good. Then you're doing just fine."

Dad stopped and leaned down and looked me in the eye.

"You have all the talent inside you to do anything you desire with life. and you have the strength inside you to get done whatever needs to be done. Fear is good. Channel it and it will help you know when the proper time is to stand up for yourself."

With that I got into his truck and made the long trip back home. The old man couldn't contain his smile. I am not sure if it was because he was proud of me or proud of himself for being strong enough to be there.

If anyone knew about true strength, it was Dad.

White Pants

As the summer after my eighth-grade year was under way, some real changes in my life were occurring. First off, I was becoming a man. I knew this because I started to enjoy R-rated movies, and I stopped wearing tight white underwear and moved into boxers instead. I took these all to be signs of impending manhood. My manhood was certainly impending, but it was also awkward at times – deflating to talk about, and often disappointing to look at.

The summer was memorable for many reasons. One was a new game we developed, called "Crack Contests," to play with the girls. The game was simple. You dove into the pool, and whoever's pants fell the most won. The flaw was that men's swim trunks were much more likely to fall than anything that the girls wore. So Dan and I modified the game to include the provision that we could stand under the diving board and grab at the girls shorts as they dove in. It was an interesting concept, but far from making the Olympic games as an event.

This was also the summer that I started to really enjoy playing the piano. I found it to be a soothing outlet to the crazy moods that I seemed to drift in and out of. No matter what mood I was in, I could sit at the keys and write something to help release the pressure that had me under constant strain. Many a summer night I would sit in the music room and play the piano as the sun sank below the horizon. The view from the bench overlooked a well-manicured backyard with a large, sparkling pool as its focal point. When I wasn't playing I would listen to the sound of restless crickets, the quiet hum of the pool motor, and the rustle of the branches in the slight summer breeze. Those nights seemed to last forever as the quiet of the house and the fervent chirping of the night critters clashed.

At this point in life, my mother would likely be in her bedroom by 9:00 P.M., her door locked. The house would be completely still as my little brother slept. Mom was prone to random fits of anger at Dad or extreme grief at the death of her marriage. Couple that with the half bottle of wine she ravaged in the evening and it was uncertain where her mood swings would take her. On many nights, it was simply to a restless sleep.

On those nights, the large house was mine. Sometimes the guys would come over and we would talk about how to get beer and convince girls to do the things that we ourselves didn't know how to do yet. Sometimes the girls would join us to swim. Sometimes it would just be Mike or Andrew or Dan. We would talk about which girl we thought we really loved. The emotions we felt could be deplorable in one moment, only to turn into deep rivers of true love the next. From day to day I truly loved Katie or Laura or Megan – or whomever else may have crossed my path that day. This love wasn't any less strong than any love I would feel later in life; it was just much more free and fleeting, like that summer breeze gently rippling through the night air.

Most nights, however, I sat at the beautiful Steinway grand. It was an exquisite instrument. The ivory keys had just the right tension when depressed and the action of the pedal was perfect. Here I poured my confused soul out. For hours at night I would tinker with music and let it sink in through my pores and resonate with some sort of tuning fork that ran the length of my body. Later in life, I would hear a certain chord of a choir or a symphonic piece, and that tuning fork would ring right through my whole body again, tingling, and if it was perfect, an unexplained tear would form in my eyes. We all have a soundtrack to our lives, a rhythm we live by. Mine was more Barry Manilow than Barry White, but I digress.

75

That summer was thick with tension. Dad had moved into a tiny no-bedroom, imitation apartment in an area of town he referred to as Felony Flats. At one point he was mugged. A gunman demanded his money, and when Dad told him that he didn't have any, the man responded, "Hey, I don't want to shoot you."

"That's too bad," Dad responded, "I would appreciate it if you did."

The gunman shook his head and walked away. He had underestimated the misery of an old drunk with new sobriety.

Mom had fallen into a deep malaise. She cried constantly and her moods were irrational. She had always been a little demanding, with a Stalin-styled regime for running the house. On more than one occasion all the men – my dad, brother, and I – were ordered into matching traditional German lederhosen as Sunday garb for church and brunch. She had the outfits made by hand by an Austrian seamstress she had met during her college year abroad. Other times, there were different themes, such as a simple sweater with our names stitched in the front.

My favorite (albeit twisted) memory might be the white pants, which are still a source of legend in my family. As a child, and later an awkward teen and adult, I was a terrible, clumsy mess. It didn't matter what it was – if it was on a plate, it was ending up on my shirt. For a while we simply matched the food to the color of my apparel, but during Mom's kelly green phase, this became terribly problematic. So until I was fourteen, whenever we went out I wore a large plastic bib that covered my body, and I even wore a hoodie, as sometimes food would end up in my hair. Better safe than sorry.

The white pants were my mother's "Man of la Mancha" moment, her windmill. Every Easter she insisted on having me wear the pants. It didn't matter how many people warned her against it or how adamantly my father argued to just put me in some asbestos siding for my own safety and relax. It was always the white pants.

Easter was spent at my grandparent's house. We would all go to mass, and then head to brunch at the club (in the white pants). After brunch (and after I had been hosed down), we would retire to my grandparents for a day of socializing. This consisted of my grandparents sucking down a bottle of Cutty Sark and talking about what a disappointment their children were and how the future was riding on the grandkids to keep the family legacy together. My parent's generation responded by drinking beer and chain smoking while secretly hoping that my grandfather had syphilis from the war and the two would need to be put in a home for their own safety. I am not sure which war grandpa was a veteran of, he looked ancient so I would guess the war of 1812.

The grandkids would happily participate in an Easter egg hunt. To keep things interesting, my grandparents used plastic eggs and placed different amounts of money in them: quarters, $1, $5 and $10 bills, and, just to ensure that there would be a hospital visit that day, one egg had a $100 bill.

As the Easter egg hunt got underway, the larger boys, all in high school, would elbow their smaller kin to the ground and laugh at how puny we were. Whoever was lucky enough to find the $100 bill was in for a severe beating. Denny was the oldest, and he was 6'8" and 290 pounds by eighteen. He would later play football at Stanford and was arrested for bull fighting. He misunderstood the sport and simply punched out as many bulls as he could. His personal record was 12.

Whoever found the lucky egg would immediately run to Denny to give him the prize in hopes that he would not twist him into the ground like a cork screw. Since a beating was more entertaining to the parents than a hug, Denny always obliged them. Meanwhile, the elder generations had action on how many of the grandkids would cry, how many concussions would be sustained, and, of course, at what time I would fall and get grass stains on my white pants. Hundreds of dollars changed hands in the course of an Easter afternoon.

If the Easter egg hunt did not spell my doom, then it would be up to the others to manufacture a way to get me to fall and entice my mother into a psychotic fit. Most the time this fell to my uncle Mickey. Mickey was the bachelor of the family and the only male offspring of my grandparents. He believed and acted as though he was the second-coming of James Bond, but he really bore more resemblance to Bond's distant cousin Mort. Suave and confident, he could charm the pants off a nun and claimed he had. Apparently, there was dust.

At Easter, Mickey would grab a football and ask if anyone wanted to play some catch. I always was ready to play, and thus my downfall. Mickey would warm me up with a few light throws.

"Okay," he would say, "run a fly pattern to the back corner of the yard. I'll hit ya."

When the ball would float over my head he would start the provoking with, "Come on, you gotta dive for that."

"I can't Mickey, Mom will get mad."

"Your mom...your MOM? Don't you worry about your mom. I'll handle her. Now I don't want to see this ball hit the ground. You hear me buckaroo?"

"Okay Mick," I would pant.

Throwing me a football is like placing an altar boy in front of a priest. It's only a matter of time until someone is on their knees.

Sure enough, Mickey floated the ball over my head and I sprung my little legs into action. I laid out and skidded on the grass ten yards, making a tremendous catch. In response, a loud cheer rang up from the gallery that had now gathered around the back yard. My Uncle Peter, with a Marlboro slapping the sides of his mouth, yelled, " I got 1:15! I got 1:15! What's the pot up to?"

His wife slammed her beer on the table. "Couldn't hold off ten minutes, not ten fucking minutes?"

With that, a bellow came from the back; it sounded like the last report of a dying buffalo. My mother charged in a similar fashion towards me on the grass. As she charged, the lashing I was about to take made the joy of a fine catch dissipate and the realization that I was in deep trouble sank in. I started to cry as my mother thundered towards me.

"Not the white pants, not the white pants."

"Come on now," my now neutered and worthless Uncle Mickey said.

"You shut up. Look what you did to the white pants."

Mom's nostrils would be flaring and her raven black hair fluttered behind her.

"What did I tell you?"

"No grass stains, Mom."

"That's right, no grass stains."

"And what is that?"

"A grass stain and maybe some blood."

With that she scooped me up and dragged me into the house to change my pants and give me the spanking that I had earned. Oh well, I had lived seven good years. I just hoped my little brother didn't find my stash of Bit O Honeys before the funeral.

At this point my mother was in such a rage that all she could do was grunt "white pants," which she repeated over and over until I was sure she was in a trance. When the fit was over I would appear from a back bedroom, and what would I be dressed in? A fresh pair of white pants. Thus, the scene would repeat itself. This went on every Easter for the bulk of my childhood.

Graduation Day

All good things must come to an end, and junior high was no different. For me, things ending involved despair and destruction, be it physical or mental. Again, junior high was no different. My dog Jazz would suffer the most.

It was June, and summer vacation was on the immediate horizon. Minds were unfocused and scattered as the school year and our junior high careers wound to an end. We prepared ourselves for the big time. Everything was bigger in high school: the football, the workload, and the girls' bra sizes. It was to be the best of times. To get there we first needed to close the chapter of our lives that was the eighth grade and prepare to move on.

Much was still unsaid; many things were still undone. We still hadn't successfully lit Bill Creswell's hair on fire during recess in order to distract the teachers long enough to shotgun the Rainer Ice beers that Dan had stolen from his garage fridge. We still hadn't planted the Penthouse magazine that Andrew took from under his dad's mattress in Walsh's desk then turn him in. In fact, we still hadn't gotten it back from Mike. The deal was that everyone had two nights with it before we planted it on F-ing Walsh. It was going on two weeks and Mike's smile had grown annoyingly bigger every day that he had it. It couldn't be the articles because Mike could scarcely read. All in all, there just seemed to be a lot to do before we all went our separate ways to high school.

Perhaps that was overly dramatic since most of us would be going to the same high school. There was only one Catholic high school in town, Prep, and most of us would continue our scholastic careers there. However, some of us would fall prey to the remedial level of public school. Who knew what would happen to those folks, as everyone knew that public schools were dens of drugs and crime. Most would enter as naïve children and exit as low level members of either the Bloods or the Crips. We knew as a group that we needed to streamline our goals for the remainder of the school year but no one knew how. Mostly because we couldn't remember what our goals had been.

It was a typical Friday night excursion when our last big plan came to us. We were toilet papering Katie's house as we had every Friday for the past three weeks and would continue to do every Friday throughout the summer, when Mike had what he assumed was a grand plan for the graduation ceremony. We should be stoned.

A little about TP-ing Katie's house: the need to send her a message started three weeks prior when she was caught making out with F-ing Walsh before school as the bus picked them up. I was also on this bus route, as we all lived about five blocks from each other, and I was offended to see my girlfriend kissing another guy. Well not another guy, but still…F-ing Walsh, and Katie didn't know that she was my girlfriend, so I didn't totally blame her. However, the guy-code dictated that she was certainly mine, as I had gone further with her than any other guy. I had gotten to third base, if you consider third base touching on the outside of the pants. To my knowledge (and let's face it, we all would have known) no one else had even really gotten to second base, let alone quasi-third. F-ing Walsh, of all people, knew this and still chose to stab me in the back by kissing my girlfriend. For the record, I also considered Megan, Laura, Samantha, and an Indian exchange student named Sumar to by my girlfriends.

Retribution for this injustice was to be swift and fierce. F-ing Walsh, who chewed Copenhagen in class, found his spitter with a hole in the bottom. His spittle leaked over his desk, lunch and pants. Katie would receive her sentence that night.

We all gathered at the corner of 29th and Bernard at 11:00 P.M., sharp. I had stolen several roles of Charmin from our basement pantry and Andrew had secured a dozen eggs. Dan brought a bottle of pink nail polish that seemed to serve no purpose until F-ing Walsh showed up. The original plan had been to egg F-ing Walsh's house after Katie's, but we couldn't do that with him standing there. So in order for him to come along Dan would paint his fingernails pink. F-ing Walsh took to it far too naturally.

F-ing Walsh's excuse for making out with my girlfriend had been solid enough to ward off a more serious punishment. As he explained it, Katie had been playing MASH, a game of chance in which it was decided that she would live in a shack, make $20,000 a month, and marry Walsh. They would have seven babies and she felt that she needed to get the work started immediately. F-ing Walsh had little choice but to comply as the woman was throwing herself at him. In guy-code, this is a completely acceptable practice depending on how good of a friend you are with her boyfriend. Since F-ing Walsh never really liked me, and I thought he was the son of an autistic simian, and of course Katie had no idea I had marked her as my territory, there was little to hold F-ing Walsh accountable for. The guy-code is pretty complex.

We all set out to toilet paper Katie's house. Twelve full rolls played about tree limbs, gutters, shrubs, and an 86 Toyota Celica that belonged to her brother. A dozen eggs smashed against the garage and front door. As we were running, we decided this was so much fun that we should do it next Friday too. So it was that every Friday for three and a half months we vandalized Katie's house. As their paper boy I saw Katie's dad out cleaning every Saturday morning at 6:00 A.M. As a proper lad intrigued with the idea of getting in his daughter's pants, I always made it a point to help clean up until he made a gesture for me to continue on my way.

"A nice young man like you needs to finish his job," he would say.

"Yes sir. I sure hope they find the hooligans that did this to you…again."

"I hope so, too. Why can't kids today be more like you? Hard working and respectful – say, how would you like to bed my daughter?"

He said something like that anyway. Maybe not word for word.

The Friday excursions were carefully orchestrated and several recon teams took charge over the summer. No matter who may have been out of town or busted by their parents for sneaking out, the job was always done. We were more organized than NASA.

So, it was decided that we would walk to receive our diplomas stoned. I had never been stoned. I was pretty nervous and paranoid on my own without the assistance of an intoxicating substance, but nevertheless I didn't want to be the only one sober. Now I don't condone buying drugs. They are needless and expensive. That's why I never buy drugs but mooch off of my friends instead. Mike felt he could get his hands on some pot. Who were we to argue? We had never seen pot, and Mike had older brothers. I think one was doing a stretch in San Quinton. If anyone could get his hands on drugs, it would be him.

The ceremony was going to take place in St. Augustine's, the schools attached church. The 42 class members of the 1991 graduating class gathered outside the entrance in the order that had been decried at the rehearsal the day before. Of these classmates, four would shame their Catholic parents by being gay. None of them would grow up to be priests as demanded by canon law. Three would die tragically before turning twenty, two while skiing. Six others would spend time in jail. One would burn his house down; one would go to jail for shooting at his four-year old son. Fifty percent were from what is termed a broken home, including me, while twenty-five percent wished that they had been adopted, and ten percent would tell people that they were. Most were Republican as children, would grow to become liberal, and then turn back to Republican after they received their inheritance. None of these stats mattered to us. What we cared about was each other. Many of the girls were already bemoaning the end of an era. Ironically, they all would be reunited in high school three months later. It didn't bother us because the girls were giving out free hugs. If I needed to cry on cue to get some physical attention, so be it.

Unbeknownst to us, Mike was having a hard time tracking down the pot. He tried to talk to Matt, as Matt was the one black guy we knew, but he said his ballet instructor couldn't score any. So Mike took some dried rosemary and some pine needles and put them in a sandwich bag. This would serve as our pot. As the others were lining up for the procession we snuck around the side of the building to a small green belt behind the gym. Mike took a diet grapefruit Shasta can and transformed it into a pipe. I was terrified, as I had heard rumors that special linings on these cans could kill you. Rumor had it that a party in Seattle had resulted in the death of six people when they used a Keystone can. I was told to stop being such a pussy and take a hit, which I did. Oddly, it tasted remarkably like my mother's spaghetti sauce. When we were finished smoking our rosemary we ambled back up to the line just as the procession was under way. Andrew and Mike couldn't stop giggling.

Let me go on record as saying I didn't feel a thing, and I said as much. F-ing Walsh, however, insisted he was high and kept banging his head on the pew in front of him as he rocked to the church music of our graduation ceremony. It was during one of these songs that I really fell for Megan. Laura, Megan, Lauren, and Samantha all sang as canters during school masses and constituted the All Saints Choir. I sang in the choir as well, making me the only guy among four attractive and eligible women. The boys of the All Saints class didn't see it that way and insisted that I was more like Matt than I wanted to admit. As the ceremony drew to a close, Megan stepped forward to sing a prepared number, "Ave Maria."

She was nervous as she stood by herself in front of a few hundred people. She smoothed down the sides of her dress with her hands and drew in a deep breath as she began with perfect pitch. The music rang from her body as gently as a summer breeze. Easily the notes wafted around the cavernous room. She closed her eyes as she sang and gently tipped her head to the side. Her blond hair was pulled back in a ponytail, but a curl broke free and drifted by her temple, floating with the music. Her rigid body slowly melted as the music rang from her very soul. My father was standing in the back of the church and his jaw dropped at the beauty of her work. Never before had I witnessed such a transforming moment. I fell in love with her, or maybe the music she created. It didn't matter; I was captured.

My mother sat with my siblings and looked annoyed, as the music was distracting her from finishing the book she was reading. When the song came to an end, the audience released the breath that they had been holding in the entire length of the song. Embarrassed by the moment but pleased, Megan quickly sat down next to me. Her cheeks were flushed and a true smile played on her lips. It was the kind of rush she would learn to crave first through music and later through drugs. She took my hand and squeezed it hard. She found my eyes and they danced with joy. In the awkward silence of the moment F-ing Walsh banged his head one last time against the pew, slunk forward softly, and then hit the floor. No one cared, not even his parents.

The party was in my garage. Much thought had been put into the proper way to make my garage appear both elegant and, well, not like a disgusting garage. This meant that we added white Christmas lights. Instead of a party what we really wanted was a dance. This was the new vogue thing. Dances allowed girls to touch us without a scarlet letter being issued. This was important because now my garage resembled a shoebox with hamsters – just a dark space with animals crawling all over each other. My mother still figured this was a real party and thus had Lola, our Russian house servant, run out and buy pizza. Lola was given a credit card and assumed that she should max it out and thus we had enough pizza to feed the Red Army. My mother threatened to have her deported, which she threatened weekly. Lola didn't speak enough English to be offended.

The motley crew buzz-sawed through the first thirty pizzas but that left another fifteen to be had. Not knowing what to do with the pizza, we boys hypothesized how many pizzas Jazz, our thirteen-year-old black Lab, would eat before throwing up. Those not rubbing up against a pubescent girl joined in the game. To Jazz's credit, she ate every piece without throwing up. Unfortunately, the next day she was unable to move her back legs and was forced to move around by dragging her body with her front two legs and whimpering. My mother assumed it was a Communist act by Lola, but the vet said it was because she had eaten too much cheese and was unable to poop it out and the weight of the gummed-up mozzarella was too much to handle. Therefore, he was forced to pull it out by hand.

As the graduation party came to an end, Mike was compelled to admit that he had lied to everyone and we had smoked a seasoning instead of pot. F-ing Walsh didn't believe him and claimed that he had been the most fucked up ever. In F-ing Walsh's defense, he had a severe concussion from smashing his head on that pew repeatedly.

The crowds slowly thinned and all the girls cried as if this would be the last time they ever saw one another. The guys played along because there was no purpose in mocking a crying girl when it could lead to some level of sympathy-petting. In the girls' defense, some of the All Saints class of '91 would go their separate ways. A few went to public school and gracefully fell out of our day-to-day life. Two went to boarding school after watching Dead Poets Society. Matt went to jail. One boy lit a kerosene bottle on fire in his living room and burned his house down. He lived, but his Dad was a member of the Parks Board and likely had him buried in a park basketball court as punishment. Either way, we never heard from him again.

A few last voices were talking in muddled tones in a corner of the garage when Megan approached me. She had let her dirty blond hair down and changed into a more casual sundress that fluttered about when she walked. She had eyeliner on, applied in an amateur, uneven line. As she neared me I stood up from my seat to greet her. She took her hand in mine and watched as she entwined our fingers together.. She then took her other hand and repeated the process.. My heart raced when she touched me. With our hands pressed together she leaned her body towards me, supporting her weight on my palms. She leaned her face in and gently closed her eyelids and pursed her lips. Then we were together. My mind's eye rose above the two of us and floated in circles as that magical kiss silenced the room. When she pulled her lips from mine, tears brimmed her eyes and threatened to spill over. She let go of my hands and wrapped herself in my feeble arms, resting her head on my shoulder.

"Don't forget me," she pleaded.

"Even if I wanted to, I couldn't."

She looked a little perplexed at me then rested her head back on my shoulder. She didn't realize that every night as I rested on my pillow it was her soft face I saw. It was her body I desired and her laugh I craved. She would be the measure of all women for me and all would pale against her until "the one."

Megan lifted her head from my shoulder and looked me in the eye, making me go from firm to jelly. My legs went from firm to jelly, you perverts.

With a twinkle in her blue eyes and a sly smile curling her lips, she left me with a statement that would haunt my hollow mind all summer: "The best is yet to come."

And so it was.

With that she turned and walked out of my life for what felt like forever. I sat down, my body quivering and spent.

The best was yet to come.

It Begins

I started my high school career that August. I was fourteen and was preparing to move my life into a small locker in the freshmen hallway in a dilapidated building. The frosh hall was in the basement and had limited lighting. Burps from the old boiler gave a heartbeat to the walls, and the tile was pooled with puddles from the dripping pipes above our heads. The floor was a dark brown, rounding out the derelict feel of the space.

Prep was the only large private Catholic high school in town. It was small compared to the public schools but still had over 800 students. It featured state of the art 1952 architecture and style and still had the original lunch ladies, who in 1952 where just coming into their 70s. By the time I arrived they were still serving chicken nuggets of roughly the same vintage. The best thing I remember about school lunches were the nachos. They were simple enough – fake cheese on stale chips. For three years I scheduled my classes as close to the cafeteria as possible so that I could purchase these heavenly treats without getting stuck in the incredibly long line that would develop.

The school also still had its original asbestos and was shaped like an H with a courtyard in the middle. It was two stories and the upper hallways were painted in a pale tan pallet. The smell was a strange mix of Pine Sol and teenage desperation. A ramshackle football field with more holes than grass sat behind the school and served as a PE classroom and practice field for all the sports.

As with all journeys, mine started with a first step. Wearing a Christmas sweater, as insisted upon by my mother on a hot August afternoon, I walked slowly and alone to the theater for freshmen orientation the day before school started. I had no idea where any of my few friends were. The theater was a mass of bodies. Two hundred kids milled about, giggling and searching for a familiar face. Too ashamed of my outfit to search, I took a seat as far back in the room as I could and curled my legs up to my chest to block as much of the frolicking reindeer as possible. A man – we would later learn that he was the dean of students and dispensed detention like Pez candies – addressed the crowd. He started with a prayer and then went through a long list of all the things that would be grounds for detention. This diatribe lasted fifteen minutes. There were a lot of rules. I had a feeling that my very existence was frowned upon and warranted J.U.G.

"J.U.G." was the fancy Catholic school name for detention: Justice Under God. I have yet to find God washing the teachers' cars, yet these adults were taller than I so I figured they must be closer to heaven and therefore an authority, at least by elevation. When the room was broken into thirds based on the amount of money your family had contributed to the coffers over the years, I figured at least I would be able to find Mike and Dan in the poor group. But alas, my family had indeed given money to the school in the past. I understand the poor group was pulled behind the gym and ordered to empty their pockets. When that didn't suffice, they were beaten until they turned over their bus passes.

My group started by getting our school photos first – thus the purpose of the sweater – followed by a tour and then locker assignments. As I got in line, a boy with olive skin and dark features stood a foot or so in front of me.

"Excuse me," he meekly stated. "Do you mind scooting back? You're stepping on my penis."

He then released a deep laugh and turned to the guy in front of him for a high five.

So this is what high school was going to be like, I thought, all penis and fart jokes. I could live with that.

After my disappointing school picture – I had huge deer-in-the-headlight eyes and a fearful expression on my face – I toured the school and ended at my new locker. Everyone had a locker-mate, as there were not enough lockers in the school to go around. Since none of my friends had agreed to be my locker-mate I was assigned one.

Lauren was her name, and she was a goddess. With dark shoulder length hair and emerald eyes, she had a fully developed body and dark, sexy, brooding makeup. She wore leather pants and a tight t-shirt that said, "Eat Me?" with a picture of a weeping cow standing over an offspring's grave. I checked the number on the slip I held in my hand to be sure that this was truly my locker. It was. Lauren was quietly unloading her school books into the locker and positioning everything so that there would be plenty of space for her locker-mate. I stood a few feet away with my mouth hanging open, not sure how to proceed. I kept opening my mouth to talk but nothing came out. I looked like a beached fish sucking at the air. Lauren leaned over to pick up more books and I squeaked. This caught her attention.

"Hello," she said nervously, smoothing her shirt.

"Uh, um," I responded.

We stared at each other for a moment, as my mouth was too dry and numb to create words. I held out the locker slip and she took it from my trembling hand.

"Oh, so you're my locker-mate. I thought I was going to get a loser." She rolled her eyes as she said this.

That stung. My brain raced for a retort.

"I don't always wear Christmas sweaters. Unless it's Christmas or my fucking mom makes me." I stomped my foot.

"Do you hate your mother? Because I hate my mother," she responded.

"Yeah. I hate her and anyone else you want me to hate."

"Do you eat meat?"

"Only if the animal has committed suicide first."

She shook her head sadly and said, "Well you might as well put it in."

"Uh, um…"

"You can put your books in the locker. I left space."

With that she pulled out a box of Kotex tampons and put them on an upper shelf.

"You can never be too cautious," she said. "I learned that the hard way, lost my favorite pair of jeans last month."

"You know I will just hold on to my books this year. No problem."

With that I turned and walked briskly away. I never returned.

The highlight of the early year was the homecoming dance. Homecoming was the first time I would ever ask a girl out on a real date. They have professional photographers to take a picture of you and your date at the dance so that you have proof that yes, someone would really go out with you. Mike, Andrew, Dan, and I sat around Dan's basement discussing this event.

"I want to be bold," said Mike. "This is the first dance. I need to take a swing at the hottest girl I can before they get to know me."

This sounded logical, as we all agreed that Mike was pretty much a creep. Mike made a list of the top three or four girls he felt had just the right mix of attractive features to be appealing and enough daddy issues in order to actually go out with him. For my part there was no doubt who I wanted to take to my first dance ever: Megan. She was beautiful, fun, and had been willing in the past to let me touch her. Plus, I knew that I wasn't the only one who saw her beauty. She was featured in much of the talk during freshman football. I acted fast and made the stumbling call to ask her, and she agreed, mostly because I called first. I was elated that she would be mine, if only for a moment, and I would have a picture to prove it. We had drifted apart some during the summer, as she spent the vacation at her family's lake cabin. When school started back up there were so many people to get to know and everything had gone so fast that I hadn't said more than a few words to her.

Homecoming at Prep was not a formal dance but rather a themed one. That year's theme was a pajama party. Back then you could have that theme. These days you wouldn't dare open that door for fear of what teenagers might choose to wear – or more accurately what they would choose *not* to wear. I was born too early.

The plan was simple: My dad would pick F-ing Walsh up and then stop at Katie's as we were going to double date. He would then drive us to Rock City Pizza and wait patiently in the car while we ate. After dinner he would drive us to the dance and then pick us up at 10:00 and drive everyone home. I would make F-ing Walsh pay as reward for allowing him to be seen with Megan and me.

Megan wore a green set of flannel pajamas and carried a teddy bear. I had pajama pants on and Dad's old bathrobe. We fit right into the Friday night dining clientele. It's funny how you remember little things but not others. I don't remember what pizza Megan and I shared, and I have no clue what we talked about, but I remember clearly when she pulled her hair from her pony tail and let it float around her face. I remember being mesmerized by how it softly landed on her shoulders and how her bangs played about her forehead. I remember how easy her laugh came when she and Katie would tell a story. It was a deep, hearty, and true laugh. Her eyes would light up and her smile would be wide, but she laughed with her whole body.

I remember how nervous I was as I walked into the dance. Megan sensed it and slowed her walk a moment. She smiled at me and held my hand to calm me. I remember how excited she was when she walked into the gym and ran over to all her friends. As they bunched up I found Andrew and Dan, and we had a quick rundown of how our dates were going so far.

Dan's date was so in awe of his stature that he had had to send her away after she spent the entire dinner running her hand over his left bicep and moaning. I guess she had longed for the touch of a man. It wasn't going to be Dan. Somehow, the complete devotion of a woman was a turn-off. I couldn't relate; no woman had ever adored me. Andrew stood awkwardly four yards away from his date. He wasn't inclined to get any closer. Andrew had done what he was supposed to do. He dressed up in his pajamas, he picked the girl up, and he took her to dinner. He danced with her the first song and now he was done with her. He didn't see the point. What he really wanted to do was talk to his friends and maybe drink a beer. His date stood watching like a dog longing for affection. She kept a safe distance away, but she needed to be acknowledged. The apparent rejection had caused severe emotional distress for her. She now questioned everything about herself. Despite the fact that she was clearly an attractive young woman with many suitors she now was feeling completely inadequate. You could see her self-confidence descend with every song that played. She would soon be at a level where Mike could swoop in. That was rock bottom. She hated her thin oily hair and she felt incredibly fat. In her mind her legs where too much like a chicken's and her ass was an ever-expanding canvas. Andrew, without saying a word, had broken her.

I remember how nervous I was when that first slow song came on and everyone knew he or she was obligated to find his or her date and dance. The room felt like a slaughterhouse. Girls dropped their heads and quietly shuffled towards their partners. But not my date. Megan bounded over to me full of energy and grabbed my arm.

"Come on baby, let's dance."

It was the most exciting sentence I had ever heard, and everyone saw us as we raced to the middle of the floor. That was worth a lot of street cred during football practice.

She placed herself tightly in my arms and we tumbled back and forth to a song that I can't recall. I can recall how warm she felt pressed against me and how I hoped I could stop time at this moment and carry it with me forever. I could smell the shampoo in her hair. With the lights dimmed and Megan entwined with me, I learned something about her. I can't explain how I knew it. Maybe when you have those few

96

moments where you are truly connected to someone you can share your secrets with them without saying a word. I learned about Megan's spirit. She was free. Where most of us are grounded and logical, she floated above us on the breeze of her freedom. She wasn't worried about what any of this meant or what would happen next. What Megan was concerned about was the moment and how wonderful this moment was. What a gift – to be able to truly feel alive without fear of what was next or regret about what had passed. She felt safe and secure in my arms and wasn't worried about my feelings or what this might mean for her social leverage. She could feel my heart beat and she reveled in the closeness of that. For that moment she was mine and I was hers. The future didn't matter and the past was gone. There was only us; there was only this.

Then the moment passed, and Megan was off. She was working the room from friend to friend. She danced with everyone that asked her. For my part I sat on the bleachers and watched. I was happy to see her so happy. I didn't mind that she wasn't dancing with me or talking with me. That was Megan. She was free and floating about the room. We danced a few more times but more often than not I would just hear her laugh or see her smile, and that was enough.

Closing ceremonies for a high school dance consisted of one last slow song for the night. Again, this is when the women walked to their slaughter with heads hung low. They felt obligated to have at least that last awkward dance with their date as thanks for a free corsage and the complimentary trip to the Olive Garden. I searched for Megan but couldn't find her. Instead I found Whitney. I had really only just met Whitney that night. She was no Megan, but then again, who was?

Whitney was pretty with straight blonde hair that she nervously twirled the ends of with her fingers. She took a liking to me and we had danced a couple of times during the absences of our two dates. As Megan was nowhere to be found, Whitney and I danced, and truth struck me. This was it for Megan and me. I would no longer be able to keep her pinned-in. She was a big fish in a big pond, and I was of minnow status. The more she became a part of the school and the more people she met the further she would drift away from me. There was so much to see and so much to do. I would miss Megan and I would watch her from afar, and if she wanted me I would be there. Until then I would hold on to Whitney or whoever else might be settling with me, for Whitney's date was floating about as well.

Not everyone marries the prince. Sometimes people settle for the duke or, in my case, the jester. It's funny what you remember and what you forget. I am sure I was sad at the realization that Megan was never really mine, but I don't remember it. I remember how she felt in my arms for that moment, our moment.

A Place to Belong

For me, high school was more than just classes. It was more than an out of date building or a gathering spot for awkward teenagers. It was a home. It was a family. I didn't have much sense of family. My parents were divorced and my little brother had gone to live with my dad. My older sister was living on her own somewhere.

My world revolved around school. The best parts of life existed during football practice and the pick-up basketball games that we played every day during lunch and after school. It was a joy to walk down the hallway and be greeted by classmates that seemed generally glad to see me. My own house was filled with an edge. I would walk through the door with my hands clinched into a fist and with a ball of fear and anger in my stomach. I was just waiting for a fight; sometimes I was looking for one. It would only take the lightest affront to spark my anger. Not knowing what to do with this tight knot of rage, I would punch cabinets and trees. Sometimes I would throw a ball against a wall as hard as I could until my body was drained. These feelings always attacked me at home, but never at school. I walked down those hallways and felt a level of peace I couldn't obtain anywhere else.

Much of my peace came from two choir classes. I had always enjoyed music and singing, and it helped ground me. I signed up for the standard symphonic choir, but after auditions, Jack Lock, the director, asked me to join a morning class that was the elite jazz choir. Twelve students, I suppose the best singers, met every morning at 7:15 before school to work on their craft. This class introduced me to vocal jazz, big band style music, and a sense of pride. I was one of three freshmen in the class. Also in the class was Megan. She had the most beautiful voice I had ever heard, so it was natural that she would slide right in to the top choir.

Mr. Lock was in his forties and had dark rimmed glasses and short black hair. Average in size, he was one of those people who didn't register when around. Not quiet, but certainly not one to draw attention to himself, he sauntered through life in a simple, noble manner. He was married and had been since two weeks after he had graduated from college. He met his wife in his freshman year in college and spent two years trying to work up the nerve to ask her out. When he did he was met with an exasperated, "Finally!" and they dated. She knew after the first date that they would marry. It was just that simple. They were good apart but better together. When Mr. Lock came to Prep he took over a choral program that hummed along but without much soul. He brought a level of respect to it, but it wasn't until my senior year that the choir would take on a high level of success.

The Prep choir would be a place of promise for me. I belonged. I never felt that I truly fit in anywhere else. I was friends with many different people but it took a long time to make close friends. Freshman year required a lot of feeling out, not just of the social scene, but also of oneself. I didn't excel in any sports, though I played on as many teams as would let me. I wasn't a very good partier, but not for lack of trying…I just didn't like the taste of beer and didn't see the point of getting out-of-control-drunk, though I did see the advantage when a member of the opposite sex moved in that direction.

I was lost – Mr. Lock saw that and reeled me in.

The first time he pulled me aside was after I broke a school record, an unofficial record previously held by Danny Murphy from the class of '89, who got kicked out of class in fifteen seconds, a record no one thought could be touched. In a misguided attempt for greatness I was determined to beat the record. I told everyone that I planned to attempt the feat in algebra class. The teacher was one Sally Schick. She was a fine teacher, caring and warm to her students, and she didn't deserve a student like me. When I was twenty years old I wrote to her, among a few others, and apologized for the grief I put her through. She had done nothing to be the target of my record-breaking attempt. I had chosen Ms. Schick's class simply because I had been kicked out a handful of times already.

Getting kicked out of class was a godsend. Most teachers simply kicked me out and I would spend the rest of the class period in the cafeteria trying to score bonus nachos. They rarely gave me J.U.G. because they didn't want the argument and the dean of students had made it clear that he didn't want the arguments either. In this way, I slipped through the cracks. It was not to my benefit. I could have used a heavy hand. But, Ms. Schick had a quick trigger with me, and that was essential to breaking this record.

Ms. Schick was an easy target for another reason: she had a button that could be easily pushed. She was the girls' basketball coach and a PE teacher most of the time. She had picked up one freshman algebra class for the extra stipend. She needed the money. She had short dark hair and wore vinyl athletic pants to school each day. No make-up ever made it to her face and at lunch she was in the weight room pounding some iron. It was the worse kept secret in school that she was gay. I don't remember anyone ever talking about it; you just knew. This would be my disgraceful key to breaking the record.

Students poured in and the room was at full attendance as rumor had spread about my attempt. A few extra bodies crammed the windowless classroom that we occupied. Walsh sat next to me with a stopwatch poised. Ms. Schick walked in moments after the bell already talking. "Open your books to page sixty-nine." Everyone giggled.

"Get a grip people," she responded.

"Walsh, start the clock," I said.

With that, I got up and walked to the front of the room. I took the dry erase pen out of her hand and quickly wrote an equation on the board. When I stepped aside from the board so the class could see it, I got the reaction I was looking for.

"Get your books and get the hell out of here."

"Time? Walsh, stop the clock. What's the time?"

"12 seconds. You did it."

"I did it!" I exclaimed raising my hands in the air. "An all-time new record. I have claimed my rightful place among the legends."

A cacophony of applause followed me out the hall as I made my glorious exit. Later in life I would recognize what a truly terrible act it was. Who knew that teachers had feelings?

I went about my day as if nothing had happened. When I walked down the hall, high-fives and kudos greeted me. I was getting the attention that I so craved.

It was Mr. Lock who reeled me in. I didn't realize at the time that teachers were humans. I just assumed they were asexual, cyborg-type beings. Once class was over I figured they went into a storage room and were shut off for the night, waiting to be awakened for class the next morning. I guess I got the idea from the show *Small Wonder*. It never occurred to me that they would talk to each other. After the lunch break, though, I was getting a lot of disgusted looks from the faculty. Mr. Lock pulled me aside.

"What you did was not appropriate. I will not have a choir student acting that way. If you want to remain a part of this class you will apologize and you will report to me after school for the rest of the week."

I couldn't imagine not being in choir. I liked it there. I was good. Megan was there. I would take my medicine.

When I reported after school I was presented with piles of sheet music of all sorts. They were all commingled together and spread across the large classroom. I would later learn he had pulled every piece of music in his cabinets out and thrown them on the floor.

"Your job," he said, "is to file all of this music by part, and then alphabetically. When that is finished you will be allowed back."

With that he went back to working on the piano. He tinkled music a few notes at a time and then would stop to write it down with his pencil. I listened intently as he wrote. He was working on a four-part symphonic piece for the Christmas concert. Something wasn't right, and he couldn't put his finger on it. I took a risk and engaged him.

"Mr. Lock, are you having a problem with that last chord?"

"Yes, it doesn't quite fit."

"What if the sopranos went up a third instead of staying on the G?"

He worked through a few of the measures and then tried the new chord.

"You're right; good ear."

With that he started to include me on the process of writing the song. Over the next week, as I filed that sheet music, I truly listened and learned how to put together a piece of music. He took my advice when I had something to add and challenged me to feel the music rather than just hear it.

"Where does the piece want to go? Do you want to allow it down that path just yet or should we wait? Music is like taking a trip. You know where you start and where to end. The question is what you want to show on the path to the end. With music, the story is the journey. The beauty of a piece of music is the passage getting there."

At the Christmas concert, we sang his song – the song he wrote – but when he introduced it he gave credit to both of us. Both my parents were in attendance, and both marveled at the fact that I had helped write a piece of choral music. Of course I hadn't written it. I had simply followed the path that Mr. Lock had shown me. He had a plan all along. He reached out. He found a way to connect with me, something that was unique to the two of us. I got the attention I craved, but also found a kindred spirit. I sang the music feeling every note and every chord, just like he suggested.

There was one suggestion I did make. I wanted a solo for a soprano. Something simple and beautiful, and there was only one person who could sing it. Megan. She sang it with wonder and beauty. It would be the first of many songs I would write for her but the only one she ever sang.

And yes, I realize how creepy that makes me sound.

The Goalpost

John C. Walsh's story is a simple one, as he is a simple man. Tragically born without common sense, he was a ticking time bomb since birth. No matter how much money his parents threw at schools, therapists, and police departments, it never changed the fact that John C. Walsh was a bit of a dumbass. In fact, that may have been his greatest quality. He was a man who would go on in adult life to flood his fiancés townhome because he passed out in a drunken midnight bath with the water running, a man who was found wandering an urban neighborhood at two in the morning (sans pants) looking to purchase a block of cheddar cheese – this was a man of moronic destiny.

F-ing Walsh threw the first great high school party. A party can only be great if it is busted by the cops and results in several citations. To this I day I do not understand why parents would leave teenage boys at home alone for a weekend. There is no possible way that the results can be positive. I heard it from parents all the time: "What I am supposed to do? Stop living my own life?"

The answer is, of course, "yes." You made that call fifteen years earlier. You could be traveling the Mexican Rivera without worry right now, but no, you had to have a kid, and that kid was F-ing Walsh – devoid of the mental dexterity necessary to understand and appreciate a situation without it having a moronic result.

Which leads us back to the party.

It started as a simple gathering, just a few friends and Walsh's dad's beer. Word started to spread; I may have invited every girl I had ever met, including Sybil Stadmueller, the German girl, who was practicing to be a nun. I had been on a horrible dry spell, and I wasn't about to let a lazy eye and a rumor about nuns-to-be having STDs dissuade me from upping my odds a little.

Of course, somebody let Joe Gaukroger know. We pleaded with him to be subtle, but Joe took to subtly about as well as he took to consensual sex – that is, he didn't understand the meaning. Once Joe knew, the world knew. The house was quickly filled with pulsating bodies from wall to wall. Over a hundred people gathered and spread out on to the grounds. Mike, Dan, Andrew and I gathered in the living room trying to devise a game plan while Walsh ran from room to room trying to keep order. It was a losing proposition for him, given that he didn't understand the concept to begin with.

"There are a lot of girls here that don't know me. That's a good sign." said Mike.

"Play it cool man, let the girls come to you. Be the honey," Dan retorted.

That was easy for Dan; he was athletic and good-looking, and he didn't have horrible dandruff and an itchy scalp. I really needed to bathe more.

"What if your best shot at a girl is that they are really drunk, and they think you're someone else?" I asked.

"That works, too."

The truth was that I couldn't get my mind off Megan. Not even seeing Katie or Laura changed my mind. I was starting to feel like a one-woman man. What happens when that one woman doesn't really talk to you anymore? Since Megan had found her social groove, grade school friends were passed by for new friends – bigger, taller, more athletic friends. Friends that didn't have dandruff flakes on their shirt or friends that had a car or didn't produce an obscene amount of spittle when French kissing (stop laughing, I get nervous).

The party had grown out of control. Beer cans were being thrown in the living room and someone had started a fire in the back yard by pulling shingles off the roof for firewood. Walsh held his face in his hands and slowly shook his head back and forth.

"What am I going to do, man? My parents are going to kill me."

"Yeah, probably. Let's face it, they didn't really like you much anyway. Seamus was the one they wanted; you were the one they hoped miscarried," Andrew encouraged. "Shit, it's over now anyhow. You might as well get drunk and have fun."

"That's a pretty good point. I need a beer."

"Take mine," I said, "I don't really like the taste. I need to see if I can find Megan anyway."

"You have to stop with Megan. Let her go, man. She hasn't talked to you in weeks. That's like ten months in high school years. She's not into you. Besides, I hear she is dating a junior. He drives."

"What should I do Walsh, just give up? Do I look French?" (The joke was lost on F-ing Walsh, naturally.)

"I'm just saying you shouldn't put yourself through this. Sure, you're fat and awkward. Sure, you might be the worst athlete on the football team and a social leper, but look around. There are dozens upon dozens of women here." He put his hand on my shoulder in concern. "They can't all possibly know that."

With that the doorbell rang and Joe Gaukroger opened the door so that Megan could walk in. She had her blond hair pulled back into a loose ponytail. She wore tight jeans with fashionable black boots and a black sweater that clung to her body.

"Come on in," Joe said to her. "Why don't you make yourself at home and clean the kitchen?" With that, Joe let out a hearty laugh that made the hair on my neck stand up. Megan rolled her eyes and walked by him. She went from room to room, greeting her friends.

"You're out of your league man," Walsh said as I stalked behind her.

As the night wore on I sat quietly on the couch, taking it all in with Dan. Dan didn't bother to get up and mingle. If anyone wanted him he would be here, on the couch. Andrew was outside playing catch with a football and Walsh had disappeared. The rumor was that Katie felt sorry for him and was willing to show him her boobs. She reasoned that as soon as his parents found out about this he would only be allowed out of the house for church; this could be last time he would have the chance to see boobs until college.

Meanwhile, Dan sat sentry on the couch. After a few moments a girl named Abby sat next to him. Abby had dark hair and muddled brown eyes. She had a tremendously large chest, almost to the point of shock. Abby had gone person to person in the room asking, "Are you Dan? I'm looking for Dan. I went to junior high with him."

She turned those muddled eyes on me. "Are you Dan?"

"Why?"

"I went to junior high with him and I heard he was going to be here."

"What's so great about him?"

She rolled her head back and closed her eyes as she pulled his image from the recesses of her memory.

"He was beautiful. I had such a big crush on him and I never told him. I suddenly have the courage."

"I hear you can get that in liquid form."

"Huh?"

"What are you going to do if you find this Dan?"

"I'm gonna mount him."

With that she stood up and let out a "whoa" and raised her beer in the air. This caused her to fall backwards and hit the floor.

I peered down at her. "Hmmm...so where did you go to school?"

"Blight."

"Public school girl. Alright!"

She turned to Dan on the couch next to me. He had taken all this in without a single twitch of a muscle.

"What about you? Are you Dan?" she slurred.

"Yes, I am," he responded coolly. As he spoke he got up and took her hand and ascended the stairs.

"Just wait, my man. Public school girls are everywhere. You'll see." Then he was gone.

I stared straight ahead. This wasn't my thing. I didn't like to drink, and I didn't really fit in. I wasn't like Dan; girls didn't look for me and throw themselves at me. I couldn't be Mike, who at that moment was trying to explain to two girls how his erection counted as personal growth. I wasn't even F-ing Walsh – no one felt sorry enough for me to take their top off. I just was, and I was starting to feel like I didn't want to be there.

I laid my swirling head on the back of the couch and allowed myself to close my eyelids. That was when I felt something on my shoulder. I opened my eyes to see that Megan had rested her head there.

"I just want to fall asleep," she said.

I didn't say anything; I just sat. Joe approached.

"Come on Megan; let's go to the fire. It's really going now that we are burning the coffee table."

"Uh Joe, I'm drunk. I just want to sit."

"I know you're drunk; I'm counting on it." He winked at her, but it looked more like he was trying to squeeze a turd out of his eye socket.

With that he pulled her up and away.

"Hey Joe," I yelled, "she wants to sit. Why don't you just let her sit?"

I was offended. The head-resting bit was likely to be the best action I got all night.

"I don't see how this concerns you."

"That's because you have a severe learning disability and are unable to put cohesive thoughts together."

He looked puzzled. I stood up.

"Megan, what do you want to do?"

"I just want to sit. My head hurts."

"There you go, Joe."

Joe let go of her wrist but now all his attention was on me. This couldn't be good. A fire brimmed behind his eyes. A couple thousand years ago he simply would have hit Megan over the head with a club and dragged her back to his cave. Now that social etiquette required that he ply her with alcohol first, the rage was settling on me. I certainly couldn't let him get me back to his cave; there was no telling what he would do to me. I may not have been able to walk for weeks.

"You looking for a fight?" he slobbered at me.

"No, I just think you should leave the girl alone."

He slapped me. "Come on, pussy."

I looked around the room, seeking some assistance, maybe a harpoon. I received nothing but blank stares.

He knew it, I knew it, and everyone in the room knew it. I was beat. I wasn't going to fight; I was going to back down. Lucky for me, the police crashed the party at just that moment.

Bodies flew everywhere in panic. I looked to Megan who was damn near passed out and grabbed her.

"You have to wake up. It's the cops."

Her eyes popped open and we were on the move. We ventured first through the kitchen to the sliding door leading to the backyard. We stopped a moment to admire the fire. It had become a beautiful night and the fire was a lovely hue. I did my best to support Megan's weight, but it was slow going. In front of me Joe flashed by and ran straight through the back fence, bringing down an entire section in one fell swoop. Dozens of lemmings followed him.

When Megan and I were a few blocks from F-ing Walsh's, we stopped fleeing. We quietly walked to Megan's; I was holding her hand to keep her from getting the spins and falling down. She lived next door to Andrew, and during the journey I didn't say a word. Neither did she. When we arrived, she simply turned back and smiled and then walked through her gate to her back porch, through the back door, and then to her room.

I sat on Andrew's front steps and waited for him to return. I watched Megan's window. A soft light popped on and I could make out her shadow as she changed out of her soiled clothes. Her outline softly swayed under the influence of the alcohol, and then her window was dark.

F-ing Walsh did get grounded for what seemed like an eternity, but that didn't dim the significance of the great party. It was the party by which all others would be measured.

F-ing Walsh survived being grounded because he was newly in love. That following Monday we were given a student teacher in English class. She was thin with brown wavy hair. She was an immediate hit because she wore low cut shirts and leaned forward in her chair as she went over the weekly vocabulary words. Walsh would stop at her desk after class and ask if there was anything he could do for extra credit. When the extra credit was exhausted, he started to walk her to her car, carrying her books or papers or anything else that needed carrying. It was sad, pathetic really, to see a man so lovelorn that he sat and just watched her. I told Andrew that if he ever caught me acting that way to just punch me to bring back some common sense. He punched me, twice, in the chest.

During PE just a week after the party, the student teacher was outside by the field watching the action and sneaking a cigarette. The class played touch football. It had been a mundane game at first, but her presence upped the ante for F-ing Walsh. He became much louder and more aggressive. A small boy, who would later join the choir, and in his twenties, a gay pride parade, caught a ball over the middle, and instead of tagging off, F-ing Walsh lowered his shoulder and drove him into the dirt. He then let out a beastly howl and pounded on his chest while stepping on the boy's skull. He had her attention.

"Dan," F-ing Walsh said in the huddle, "Throw me the ball. I'm going deep."

"Okay, okay, whatever."

"No Dan, its important. Throw me the ball; I will catch it."

F-ing Walsh had rare determination in his eyes. Too bad he had borderline palsy in his DNA.

Dan dropped back to pass. Walsh plodded off the line and started a post route, a deep route. Because F-ing Walsh was so fucking slow, Dan had to avert the rush and was flushed to his right. He planted his feet and patted the ball twice before uncorking a 40-yard strike towards F-ing Walsh. We all stopped and turned to watch the ball in flight. It was beautiful. The ball arced towards the blue sky while F-ing Walsh was at full gear trying to track it down. It found F-ing Walsh's hands in the back of the end zone mere steps before he smashed full speed into the goal post.

The reaction was not of immediate concern, but of amusement. F-ing Walsh was down, and it was hysterical. He bellowed out in pain as we all ran towards him. The class circled around.

"Did I catch it? Did she see? Get out of the way, I don't think she can see me."

"You should probably be more concerned about the fact that your leg bone is sticking out of your jeans," I responded.

"And no, you dropped it. Fucking Walsh," Dan said. Walsh's leg was at an awkward angle, clearly a compound fracture. He would spend the next several months on crutches. Word of the accident quickly spread throughout the school and students started to press their faces to the windows facing the field.

When the ambulance pulled him away, the reaction was one of mirth. Yeah, F-ing Walsh was cocky and a bit of a blowhard, but we were a bunch of jerks to laugh so hard at his loss of a limb.

After the surgery, Walsh's parents reduced his grounding. They spent his inheritance on a new roof. It was a great party.

Sophomore Year

Every Tuesday afternoon over the summer months between freshman and sophomore years, my mother drove me to a counselor who listened to my perceived problems and injustices. I wasn't shy about all the things that bothered me. I spread them out on the table like an elegant buffet. The truth was that I had horrible grades, I was consistently in trouble at school, and I sometimes smoked cigarettes. I also had gotten caught throwing a party when my mother was away. I was angry all the time that I was at home and I often looked for fights. On the other hand, I had found a place in music that I hadn't ever felt before and I was starting to believe in myself as a person. I was looking forward to my sophomore year of high school. The counselor would listen to my stories and shake himself awake when I seemed to reach a lull and he felt compelled to ask a question.

Over the course of several visits, a pattern emerged. I was angry, my mother was angry, the dog was angry, and the staff at home stole the good silver. Something needed to change. He was worried that I was turning more and more inward and letting the anger take over. He worried that my mother's pain at her divorce was being projected onto me. More importantly, he was terrified that her check might bounce. He spent some time with my parents and my siblings, and then one afternoon just a few days before football practice started he contacted both my parents and told them that he was recommending that I move in with my father.

This hit Mom like a meat clever. It was one thing to be rid of me, it was another to lose me to the other side. Instead she opted to go with another eloquent solution that had been presented to her. A family friend had overheard all the trouble I had caused and suggested that I follow in the path that he had taken: military school. If I needed discipline then, by God, this was the place for it.

She broke it to us as Dad was picking me up for the weekend. I needed to pack my shit because Monday I would be shoving off. With that, she scurried to her room. Neither of us knew what to say, so we said nothing. I am not sure either of us believed it was true. I was fifteen and too chubby for military school. I hadn't broken any serious laws and besides, being generally regarded as a smart-ass kid with very little practical future, military school didn't seem like a logical destination. Over the course of the weekend Dad and I chatted about all sorts of things, being careful to avoid the elephant in the room: why didn't I just live with him?

Dad had just started a new job. He left the world of selling agricultural fertilizer (you know, cow shit) to selling rock-crushing equipment. Not only was this job a real step up in the sales world, but it also came with a company car, gas card, and a pay raise. He was giddy at his new prospects. The only down side was he would be on the road two weeks out of the month and would miss some of the doings of his kids. He had asked us permission to miss these events and of course we agreed. This was a big time in his life.

By Sunday morning, I hadn't decided how much of a fight I was going to put up to avoid going to this new school. I didn't like the idea of leaving all my friends, but it did sound like an adventure. I would be away from an angry household and exploring the Texas landscape. I wasn't opposed to the military by any stretch; I just didn't see myself as a militant type. I wasn't one who did well with instruction, mostly because I would zone out before the instructions had been completed.

That Sunday afternoon Dad, my brother and I went to see Forrest Gump. A fine film – what I recall the most (aside from Jenny being a stripper and that there was a box of candy) was that there was honor for Forrest in military garb. Not only that, but he found a best friend and a purpose while serving. These were issues I was looking to resolve. As a fifteen-year-old boy I was searching for myself. Who was I? What kind of man would I become? What is a Brazilian, and why did I want to see it? These questions served as the backdrop to my conscious stream of thought. By the end of Forrest Gump I was convinced. I too wanted to own a shrimp boat.

That Sunday, as I was packing my bags at Dad's small imitation apartment to return home, he finally broached the subject.

"You don't have to go. You can live here," he said.

"What about your new job?"

"I can get my old job. We will be fine."

"No, you are really excited about this new job."

"You mean more."

"No Dad, I want to go. If I don't do this I may never understand what is so special about the name Jenny."

Though he felt guilty about it, he was relieved. He was willing to put his new job aside for me but he really wanted that job. I think on some level he felt it would be ok, maybe even best for me. For my part I had no intention of taking this success from him. This man struggled every day with overcoming his addiction. He was learning to build his life again brick by brick and he needed that job to rebuild. Plus I was tough. I could handle this. If this was what my mother was going to do to punish me and to punish my dad, I would show her up. You could knock me down, but I was not going to stay down. I wouldn't be defeated.

It was Krissy, Mike's little sister, who I told I was leaving. I didn't tell anyone else. That afternoon was flush with heavy, brooding clouds overhead. They had rolled in quickly. I was standing in my front yard throwing a football into the air and catching it. I escaped this way, trying to pull my thoughts apart and organize them cleanly in my mind, push away my fears and play make-believe. Throwing that football in the air I could pretend I was the star QB at Prep about to score the winning TD and the hottest girl. As I stood there all I could do was replay the visions of my school, my friends and my life. In a few hours, I would be in the air, leaving them behind. I would never return. That boy would be left in that yard.

Krissy was riding her bike by the house. She had been at the store picking up some school supplies and a new backpack. She would start high school in just a few days and her eyes danced with the excitement of it all. She placed the bike down and sat next to me on the front step.

"Hi," she said.

"Yeah, hi. Got some good stuff there?"

"No cigarettes if that's what you're asking."

"No, I don't need your smokes."

"Mike's always stealing my cigarettes."

"Your brother rapes farm animals. I am leaving, Krissy, for Texas."

"Why? For what?"

"I am being sent to military school. My mom hates me."

"Military school? But you have such soft skin."

"Thanks, I use Lubriderm and some baby oil."

"When are you going to be back?"

"End of the school year, I guess."

With that the heavy clouds gashed open and emptied their bowels. The water came down in heavy bucket loads. We scrambled up to the porch seeking cover.

"Well," she said taking my hands into hers and staring up into my eyes, "Maybe you will lose some weight?"

"Thanks."

The downfall lightened up and Krissy got on her bike and left. She looked back over her shoulder, flipping her hair, smiled, and waved.

Even as I walked towards the plane that Monday afternoon, I was not sure this wasn't just some game being played. Even with my one-way ticket in hand I felt this wouldn't happen. It wasn't until the plane ascended into the fluffy gray clouds that it started to sink in. I was leaving my life, the only one I had ever known, and entering a whole new world. I had no friends, no family, no Megan, no money. I was truly alone to face a monster of fear, my own. That monster would only grow.

At the end of the previous school year Mr. Lock had given me a tape of all the concerts the choir had performed. It included what had been my defining life moment so far – my solo rendition of "Hey Baby." As I broke into my moment, I added the flair of black sunglasses and some hip gyrations. I had tried to imitate Elvis but I was told I was more Costello then Presley. The tape also included some beautiful choral music including "River in Judea," Franz Biebl's unparalleled "Ave Maria,", Morten Lauridsen's tender "Contre Qui, Rose," and Elizabeth Posten's "Jesus Christ the Apple Tree." Jack Lock taught every member of choir "Jesus Christ the Apple Tree." It was a haunting song that spoke of Jesus as a tree that provided shelter and food. It was a simple piece that held its beauty in its simplicity.

I played the tape over and over as I headed toward the Texas skies. I was afraid and nervous, but more than anything, I was sad. I loved this music and all it represented. It was shelter and hope, beauty and love. The choir was an outlet for my energy and a social place for my friends. There, every day, I could watch and listen to Megan; I could laugh with my buddies and be inspired by a mentor. Now, I was so alone.

I landed in the middle of a sticky Texas night. At home the thermometer would be hovering at a pleasant evening cool, but here, even in the dead of night, the warm air was heavy with moisture and caused my clothes to cling to my torso. It was still in the high seventies. South Texas was hot and humid and might as well have been a new planet to me. It was just a hair past midnight as the van brought three other scared boys and me to the campus.

The buildings loomed large and imposing in the night air. It all seemed so surreal. I was quietly led into a room with two beds, "racks" in military parlance. A boy with a shaved head and fair skin quietly snored in one rack; the other was left empty waiting for my arrival. The dorm was quiet; I could hear the soft sound of my own breath. A single sheet was folded on a clean, thin mattress. The walls of white cinder block gave a cold feel to the room, enhanced by a naked light bulb that hung over a dripping sink. I turned on my Walkman and found the right position to rest as a thought played over in my mind repeatedly, "What have I gotten myself into?"

I had a fitful, frightened sleep. I woke several times. At one point I turned that Walkman back on to help ease my racing mind and lose myself in the soothing sounds of the choir music I knew by heart, the music that brought me back home. In time I would wear that thin tape until it broke from being over-played. Several times I taped the pieces back together with scotch tape and resumed its use. On this night, "Contre Qui, Rose" whispered in my ear.

"Against whom, rose,
Have you assumed these thorns?
Is it your too fragile joy that forced you
to become this armed thing?
But from whom does it protect you, this exaggerated defense?
How many enemies have I lifted from you
who did not fear it at all?
On the contrary, from summer to autumn
you wound the affection that is given you."

The French poem that Morton Lauridsen turned into a delicate piece of music was able to transport me to Megan. The words fit her so well, and maybe myself as well. It seemed that the more and more we pushed those away who care for us in order to protect ourselves, the more we damage ourselves. Megan's eyes seemed to gather distance each day. Why these thorns, rose? I could see her face and feel the heat from her touch in my mind's eye. I hoped that over the year I would not forget what her smile looked like or the power of her stare.

121

She would see me through this time. As I drifted to sleep I held the picture of her in my mind as tightly as if she lay in my arms. She would give me strength.

The school would prove to be just as frightening as I thought it would be. This fat, rich, smart-ass kid had a challenging road in front of him. Those around me proved to be hardened by life. Much of the experience was a nightmare. In my sleep, the others would come and beat me because I didn't belong, or maybe just to be mean. I was stolen from and humiliated by the others. The school was run not by the adults, but by the strongest and meanest of its students. I quickly learned to survive; I would need to be tougher. I chose to learn boxing, and over time I learned how to protect myself. I was able to fend off my attackers. My mental toughness was challenged daily, but I learned to adapt.

I only broke once. My tormentors, those who didn't like me, finally found a way to get to me. I decided early on that I would never let them see me break down and cry. No matter how hard they hit or what they may think of to rip me apart, I refused to give them the satisfaction. The one salvation of such a place is letters. little pieces of the world you left behind, the loved ones that consisted of home. Krissy wrote me often. She kept me informed of the goings-on of Mike, Dan and the rest. Per my request, she sent pictures of any girl at Prep who would allow it. Almost daily, I would read about the football team or choir. She reminded me in each letter what it was I was fighting to return to. The most important letter, though, was the first I received. At the Academy, each day lasted a lifetime. There was no peace. In what felt like my darkest hour, a letter from Dad arrived. A line reached out and grabbed my guts and made them wrench with sickness.

"I can't believe how much I miss you. I lost my best friend," he wrote.

122

He had never said anything like that to me. Sure, it was easy to say that he loved me, but it never occurred to me that he liked me, that spending time with me was as rewarding to him as it was to me. The sadness in his letter had a profound impact on me, and I read it over and over. I placed the three-pages in my sock and for a week it traveled with me. It was a part of every mile that I ran and every pushup I did. It was under my pillow as I slept.

One night when the goons who preyed on the newly arrived went door to door. They came to my door. They hit me and hit me but didn't get the reaction they desired: anger and fear. Instead the resolve of my chin forced them to change tactics. They knew how much the letter meant to me, so they took it and burned it. They laughed as the letter burned. All my emotions – the fear, the loneliness, the sadness – came to the surface and suddenly felt overwhelming. A heaviness pressed upon my shoulders, and I couldn't hold the tears back. They laughed and mocked me, but I couldn't stop my sobs. I was alone again.

What hurt the most was a phone call. After six weeks the new students were allowed to use the phone. I scrambled to it to call home and plead to return. My mother answered on the third ring. I pleaded my case, told her about the broken ribs I had suffered when someone hit me with a lock in a sock. I told her about how raw my skin was from when they had held me down and ran steel wool pads over my body.

Her response?

"You're strong. You can get through this. It's just so quiet and peaceful, I don't walk in the door each day angry, ready to fight. You will be fine. I won't bring you home. It's for the best for all of us. I need this. We need this."

Nothing hurt me in Texas more than that call. I felt my mother had deserted me. In time I would harden like the others and learn to survive, become a man. I had Krissy's letters, dreams of Megan and many other girls, and a desire to return home, unbroken, to encourage me to survive. I wouldn't let the Academy break me.

Maybe in the end my mother was right. I came home a man, a fighter. It isn't easy to make a man. When my classmates looked in my eyes they saw one thing, the boy who left was gone.

Unloading a Burden

For my junior year, I found myself back at Prep. I returned home from south Texas with more confidence in myself. I knew what it felt like to be lost without a compass, and I was determined to straighten-out and follow a proper path. What surprised me was how I responded to my friends and how they responded to me. The person who returned was in better shape and had a stronger profile than the boy who left. I was not the follower, but someone who was willing – and able – to lead.

The first time it occurred to me that I was no longer the boy I was before was just a few days after my return. A longtime friend had come over to see me. We sat quietly watching TV, occasionally tuning into the scrambled adult channel. There were moments when the TV scrambling would right itself and we would catch the occasional breast.

The friend, Zeke, had been an interloper in most social situations. He had bounced from school to school after being expelled. A classic bully, he was a windbag of false toughness. He talked as if he would fight the whole world at once and intimidated those weak enough to allow it. I used to be one of those. He had always degraded me to keep me in place beneath him. At the Academy, there had been hundreds of these guys. After a while, I had learned to keep my distance, and without anyone to believe that they were tough they tended to shrivel into dust and blow away. I should clarify – they ceased to exist to me.

But here was Zeke, unaware that our relationship had changed. I sat quietly and tolerated some of his belittling remarks and stories of toughness. I didn't respond, just kept focused on the TV. I had learned to let the air blow over me like a warm summer wind. This irritated him, and he slapped me in the back of the head.

"You listening to me?"

Without thinking I grabbed him with both hands by the throat and shoved him up against the wall.

"You don't touch me, you understand? You don't touch me."

He wiggled his body under my hands, forcing me to apply more pressure. "You're all talk, Zeke. The tough ones never talk. I hear a guy like you talk and I know I don't have to worry about you. You're soft. The tough guys are quiet. They observe."

Zeke's eyes started to bug out of his head. He tried to squirm out of my hold, but I planted the heel of my palm into his chest pressing him back against the wall.

"The tough guys don't need to tell everyone just how tough they are. You touch me again and I'll show what kind of guy I have become."

With that I let him go and sat back down. Zeke was quiet for a moment.

"Jesus, I was just joking around with you."

"Get bent."

With that he left, and I never really heard from him again. I had nothing to offer him if I wasn't going to idolize his toughness. Zeke would later land in jail after bringing a gun to a fistfight, the ultimate move of a coward.

I was surprised by my actions. It wasn't uncommon for me to be on guard in Texas, but when I got home I fell back into the easy rhythms and patterns of my past. I hadn't been sure that I had it in me to stand up to those who had ruled my life with intimidation and fear. Maybe I *was* a fighter.

This new confidence rang through me and those who saw it viewed me differently. Suddenly the popular crowd was chatting me up. The football coaches thought that maybe I had something to offer. I was different. Mr. Lock, who was also the linebacker coach on the football team, noted, "You're not soft like most of these kids. You have an edge."

This proved valuable on the football field. I saw my playing time increase, and I integrated myself into the team. I was moving on. I still saw Dan and Mike, but I seemed to be spending more time with friends from the team or the choir. The team gave me a place to channel my anger and frustrations while the choir was a place to reflect and create. The community was serving me well. Girls noticed this change. I was still not a candidate for best looking, but confidence went a long way.

This brings us to Angela. Angela was a senior and a cheerleader. At Prep, all of the cheerleaders were seniors and there were only twelve in total. They were striking in appearance. They had to be in order to make staring at them in their short little outfits worth attending a game – and of course fund-raising started at the games.

Angela fit the mold. She had creamy brown skin and short black hair that framed her face. She had riveting dark eyes, and her body was a perfect balance. She was so soft in so many ways, so different from me. I doubted she had to comb the hair out of her soap like I did.

The whole event took place on a choir trip. The jazz choir went to an area university to compete with other high schools in a vocal competition. For those who have not been a part of choir, you may be surprised to learn that I found these events far more catty, angry, and competitive than any football game I played. The twelve of us got into a van and Mr. Lock drove us the two and a half hours towards the festival. I hadn't spoken much to Angela at this point. She had joined the jazz choir in the year I was away, and we hadn't made much of an impression on each other, so you can understand why I was surprised when she sat next to me on the van and even more surprised when she rested her pretty head on my shoulder and drifted off to sleep.

When we arrived it was still well before lunch. We had shoved off in the wee hours of the morning and most of us had slept on the trip down. Now my mates roused from their slumber and started to pull themselves together. My dad arrived shortly before noon and our first performance. He brought with him enough sub sandwiches for everyone, including Mr. Lock, to feast on, and Angela and I stole away some time to eat our lunch together.

Dad attended trips like these often in my final two years of high school. Being on the road as much as he was, he found it a challenge to catch my entire schedule of games and concerts, so he planned a sales trip to whatever area of the state we were performing in whenever possible. This became a tradition for us. He himself was the son of a music professor and had grown up playing the trumpet. Here was something through which we could quietly connect. I took great pride in the fact that he was the only parent to join us.

Our first performance had its moments, and I struggled with a scat jazz solo. The soloists were chosen during the song, and I had no chance to prepare myself. A scat solo is just a rhythmic interruption and improvisational opening in the music, similar to a saxophone solo during a jazz quartet. Lock chose me to reward my dad for the sandwiches, but his choice really punished all of us. Instead of sweet music I produced a shrill tweet that lacked both rhythm and lyric. It surely cost us with the judges. However, Megan saved us once again with her chilling solo, "I'll Be Seeing You."

A favorite of hers, she seemed to channel the longing of the music, a song written from the view point of a lonely wife who sees her husband in all her memories of their times together while he is away at war. Megan never failed to nail it. She was striking in both the strength of her voice and the outer beauty she portrayed. What gave her performance even greater depth was how the song poured from her soul. Of course, I knew to whom she was singing – her father, a distant man who now seemed a shadow in her life. He was very close to her as a young girl. Playing the role of doting dad, he seemed to lose interest as she grew older and the more she grew to look like her beautiful mother.

Megan's house had become cold and sterile. The love that had once touched all three lives had turned robotic and routine. All the right words were said, and correct customs followed but without the chord of truth. I was at Andrew's one Christmas morning when I observed them. Andrew lived next door to Megan, and I spent the night with him as my mother and sister had stayed a few extra days on their ski trip in Aspen. Andrew's window looked into Megan's and also had a bird's eye view of the living room. Often, we stared at Megan's window curtain, hoping to see it flutter for us enough to glimpse Megan changing (with hopes of glimpsing – well, you know). We never had much luck. However, on this Christmas morning, we watched as the family opened gifts. Though the clothes were held to each chest, and the proper "oohs" and thanks took place, it seemed to lack the true pop of reality, as if it had been painted on a canvas rather than truly existed. It was two-dimensional. I believe Megan would search to find that tenderness and connection all her life. To add another dimension, she would drink or take drugs to mask the big empty hole that was her soul.

Singing brought her glimpses of the soul that lay dormant inside her. Where for me it was an escape, she could connect with the music. When she sang "I'll Be Seeing You" she was majestic, for she could truly convey the haunting words. She, like me, had grown up too soon.

A festival worked like so: a school group performed and was scored by a panel of three judges. After the performance one of the judges would come and adjudicate the group, that is give feedback on what needed to be improved. After the performance, the group would then sit and watch its competition perform. This is where it is vital for the spectators to tear apart everything about the opponent.

"Ugh, did you hear that pitch? What is she, a mating whale?"

"Well she certainly is the size of a whale."

"Yeah, did you see the size of her ass? It could feed an entire Peruvian soccer team."

"No kidding. Are we at a festival or the shooting of a National Geographic video?"

"How about that tenor? If he was any gayer he'd be an alto."

"That bass has all the rhythm of a Tourette's patient."

After the catty portion of the event, we would be asked to return to the stage to perform again for another set of judges, and the cycle would repeat. The choirs with the scores in the top two of their division performed in the night show in front of all the participants for the trophy.

On this occasion, I left the auditorium to visit with Dad. We went to his truck and grabbed a football to play catch. We threw the ball around and chatted about school and work and anything else that we could think of. It was really pleasant. That is, it was pleasant until I threw the ball on a rope, leading Dad to his right a little too far and he ran into a bus, gouging a huge chunk out of his shoulder. It would leave a nasty scar to remind him of his parental commitment to me.

While my father sat bleeding, Angela approached. She had changed out of her black pants and peach shirt that was the choir uniform (also a guarantee to keep down any sexual desire – the suspenders sealed the deal there) and was now in a pair of tight jeans and a revealing white tank top. I wasn't the only one who noticed; a group of young men from Rogers High School walked by as Angela leaned over.

"Hi, baby," one said, with a wry smile on his face and his eyes glued to her chest.

"Hi, sweetie," she replied, winking moments before he struck a parking sign that opened a large gash over his eye. Angela started rolling with laughter, but the boys brought it to a boil as Casanova rolled on the ground in pain clutching his face. It would take six stitches to close the wound.

Angela had always been flirtatious and forward. Her clothes were usually tight and revealing, and she had a puppy dog look that could melt men. She was prone to baby talk to get what she wanted, when she wanted it. Now between sets she sat next to me as I was resting my eyes under the shade of a small maple tree. I could feel the sun warm my skin as I rested. She didn't make a sound at first, just rested her head on my chest. I guessed that this is how older women were; they were just forward. I hadn't really talked to her before, just admired her from afar. Her bubbly nature had an allure to most men, and I always figured she belonged to the seniors. Yet here she was, resting, her body pressed against mine. She looked up at me and grabbed my eyes with her own.

"I've been thinking," she started.

"Yeah? I don't smell smoke."

"You're funny. I like that about you," she retorted while circling her fingers on my flabby, misshapen chest. "I think you should be my boyfriend."

Without thinking I responded, "You know I can't do that."

She dropped her head. "Oh, okay."

Her eyes dropped to the ground. She wasn't often rejected, and it added to her teenage insecurity. She quietly rested her head back on my chest. She listened to the rhythm of my heartbeat as it picked up speed. Her fingers now circled by my waistband.

After a few moments, she raised her head and grabbed her breasts in both hands. They spilled out of her palms.

"Did you know I have the exact same size chest as Sharon Stone?"

This caught my attention.

"Really?" I asked, my eyes glued to her heaving chest. The statement had taken the wind from me. Clearly those could be my hands.

"Yup. 34C."

"Wow."

"Well, I guess I understand how you feel."

With that she got up and walked away swinging her hips as she went. Obviously, the blood had rushed out of the majority of my body and gathered at one centralized location that left me light headed.

Why couldn't I be her boyfriend? It had just jumped out of my mouth. I didn't have a girlfriend. In fact, I had yet to have one in high school, unless you counted Copper from military school who worked hard to make me his girlfriend. I guess I figured I was waiting on Megan. Why? She had barely spoken to me except for a few pleasantries since freshman year. She hadn't written me back when I was in Texas. Why couldn't Angela's hands be my hands?

The choir was awarded a place in the night show after our second performance. This promised us at least second place. In between the afternoon performance and the evening finals we stopped and checked into a motel, the type located just off the local freeway, and then walked to a small diner across the street for dinner. As I stood at the crossing Angela came up, took my hand, and smiled. I didn't pull my hand away. This didn't go unnoticed by Megan, who rolled her eyes but said nothing.

After dinner, a meal that included Angela placing my hand on her thigh under the table, we returned back to the motel to prepare for the final performance. All was quiet, and my nerves were stretched taut when Megan pounded on my door. She pulled me aside and implored me to, and I quote, "gently remove your head from your ass."

"What are you talking about, Megan?"

"Angela. What are you doing?"

"Hopefully I am getting to second base?"

"Angela is a skank. I am not sure what she is up to, but she's playing you."

"What do you care? You don't even like me."

"I am your friend."

"Some friend. You barely talk to me; you never hang out with me. I wrote you all the time last year and you didn't write me back, not once."

"I wrote you; I wrote." She said this as she lowered her eyes to the tips of her shoes.

"I will be fine Megan."

She turned and walked slowly away. She stopped at the door and smiled. "Good luck tonight," and then she was gone.

Megan was unbelievable during the night show. She had two solos and was perfection on both. She won "soloist of the festival" and the choir was awarded first place. After it was announced, my eyes searched immediately for Megan. We locked gazes, but the moment was broken as Angela jumped into my arms in excitement. She wrapped her legs around my torso and raised her fists in the air. It was starting to look like I was the big winner that night. My groin agreed with a sudden rush of blood.

The plan was to sleep at the motel, depart first thing in the morning and be home by lunch. It was already ten o'clock by the time I settled back into my room. My roommate was quick to disappear and report to a room that had beer already on ice. I jumped into the shower and did my best to sort out what had happened.

To recap: A sexy senior cheerleader was throwing herself at me and no one, me included, could understand why. Megan had reached out to me but only because she didn't like the idea of Angela snuggling up to me. Why? She must know how I felt about her? Didn't she? She could have me whenever she wanted. All she had to do was snap her fingers, which was easy for her, but I lacked the dexterity to pull it off, especially in rhythm. As the water poured over my skin I couldn't help but wonder what the hell was going on.

Wrapping a towel around me, I left the bathroom, caught in a fog of thought. I dropped the towel and pulled on some underwear and a t-shirt. It was then that I saw a shadow move across the wall. Oddly I saw no reflection in the mirror. This is what we call foreshadowing, kids. I hadn't noticed that Angela had slipped into the room and was sitting at the edge of the bed. She stepped behind me and wrapped her arms around my chest and rested her cheek on my back.

My body stiffened. All of it.

"Angela, I don't know…I'm not sure I want you here."

"Why not?"

"I'm not sure…"

"Don't you like me?"

"Not really. I mean, I don't really know you."

Angela leaned back, her short hair framing her cunning smile. Her lips pouted.

"Oh, well don't you think I am pretty?"

"Yes. You're stunning, but I may not be the best judge. I just spent ten months with 500 guys. My blood pressure rises when the wind gusts just right."

I couldn't take my eyes off her. She had changed into flannel Hello Kitty pajama bottoms and had a clean white t-shirt that plunged at the neck. I couldn't help but think about the similarities she had told me about between her and Sharon Stone.

"I think the real questions is,", I began, "why are you here? In my room, with you know… me?"

"Because you're handsome and you're funny and smart. I have watched you from afar and seen how you are with girls."

"Yeah, how is that?"

"You protect them. You watch over them. You're safe. I have been with too many guys who are jerks. I want a nice respectful guy who will watch over me."

"Oh."

"What is it you think I want from you?" she asked, still pouting.

"I don't know…" I then lowered my eyes and whispered, "Are we trying to have sex?"

With my emotions totally exposed, Angela laughed a hearty sincere laugh.

"Oh, babe. Sex is just sex. It doesn't mean a whole lot."

"If it doesn't mean anything, then why is it all I think about?"

Angela got up from her perch and put her hands on my face, drawing my wandering eyes to hers.

"Sex is great, but intimacy is better."

"I don't want to have sex," I said.

Even as I said it, I couldn't believe the words coming out of my mouth. Somewhere inside of me came an anguished scream from my penis, "WHYYYYYY?"

"Okay," she said. She then walked to the bed and pulled the sheets back. I stood dumbfounded, watching her body work. She reached over and turned off the lamp, leaving just the ambient light off the street pouring in. She took my hand and pulled me towards the bed.

"Just lie down and relax."

I climbed into bed, and she wrapped herself around me. I could feel her chest rise and fall with each breath. I matched its rhythm. I could smell the soft lavender lotion she had on.

She was so soft and warm. I was most definitely *not* soft. This interaction had affected me in a very physical way.

I wasn't sure what she wanted from me. Was I supposed to kiss her? What if tried to kiss her and she didn't want that. Would she leave? I didn't want her to leave. This was awesome.

"Is it Megan? Is that why you don't want to be my boyfriend?"

"Why do you say that?"

"Come on," she said, turning her head and meeting my eyes, "I see how you look at her. You can stop holding your breath, by the way."

I exhaled loudly.

"I have been in love with her since grade school."

Angela let this sink in and didn't speak for several moments. "So, she is the one for you, the one by whom you will judge all others."

I didn't say anything. I just felt her heart beat against my chest.

"She doesn't deserve you. You are too good for her."

"Why do you say that?"

"Because it's true."

With that she fell quiet. Her breathing stopped its jagged edges and rounded into a gentler rhythm. I couldn't believe how wonderful it felt to hold Angela. All I could keep thinking was, "Why?" Why was she here with me? I didn't feel like I deserved this. I listened to her heartbeat. I felt her breath and was amazed as we timed up so that our chest rose and sank in unison.

As the night passed, there were two other problems: I couldn't sleep because she was crushing my arm, and it hurt like hell, but I didn't want to move and wake her, and I had a full erection. It was going on four hours. Wasn't there something dangerous about that?

At 2:00 A.M. a phone call came in from another room. I picked up and Angela, thankfully, moved off my arm so I could answer.

"What kind of bee makes milk? Boobies!" was all the caller said before hanging up.

It may have been Mr. Lock, but I am guessing not. These "booby" calls came in every half hour, keeping me awake and at full tilt as Angela snuggled ever closer, pressing her soft body against me. At 4:00 A.M. a haggard knock sounded on my door. I slowly got up and did my best to think about Rosie O'Donnell naked to ease the blood flow. After a few moments, I was flaccid enough to at least hide it by pushing "it" up into my elastic waistband. I opened my door to Megan.

I stepped outside so as not to disturb Angela. Megan was drunk and had stains from tears on her cheeks. She threw her arms around me in an embrace and then nearly fell over, almost taking me with her. She was very drunk.

"You know I have a brother?" She drawled. "He is a couple years older than me. I haven't seen him in four years. He just left. He left me alone with my parents, my loveless, bastard

139

parents. He doesn't call on my birthday or come to Thanksgiving dinner. He is just gone. Someday I will just be gone, too."

She looked into my eyes.

"You should come with me."

"Megan, let's get you to your room."

"I am drunk," she slurred.

"Clearly."

We wove our way down the hall and into her room.

I pulled her into the bathroom and held her hair back as I made her vomit the poison out by putting a toothbrush down her throat. She would thank me in the morning. Remnants had landed on her shirt. I walked her to the edge of her bed and sat her down. I pulled the offensive shirt off and found another. I pulled it gently over her head and tucked her between the crisp sheets. I turned off the light and sat beside the bed, listening for her to drift away to sleep.

"Why do you take care of me?"

"It's my calling."

"You're good at it. You always have been. I know you are always there for me."

"And yet sometimes you don't want me there."

"That's true," she responded, "sometimes I don't. But sometimes I need you and you're there. I love you, you know. For watching out for me."

"Well that's something, I guess."

"I hate my parents."

I stroked the hair from her cheek. "I know. Just go to sleep. I'm going to leave these Tic Tacs by your bed for the morning. Use them."

"Will you be here in the morning?" she asked, as she drifted off.
"I will be here for you. I'm always here for you."

"And that's what makes you a sucker," she said, and then she was gone.

I stumbled back to my room. Angela slept quietly. I woke her as I climbed back into bed. She pressed herself against me and smiled. Then she parted her firm lips and kissed me. Once again, I was too rigid to move. The erection would last all through the ride home as Angela sat next to me. Hours of blood flow had gone to my groin and when I stood I felt immense pain. It was as if someone was stabbing me in the testicles. I tried helping unload the bags and drum equipment, but every step I took felt like a midget was using my balls as a piñata. I took very small deliberate steps hoping that no one noticed. I guess a 14-hour erection isn't good for you.

Angela would quickly break up with me just like Megan had said. We spent a week and one Valentine's dance together before she left me for a taller senior, Rex. He was a wrestling champ. It was the most painful break up I had ever felt. I sat for days in my dark, empty room listening to Journey music.

My mother called me pussy-whipped and told me to grow a pair. If I was going to be pussy-whipped I might as well have gotten some pussy. Instead, I just held the memory of my first intimate night with someone and felt the stabbing pain of the death of it. This made Megan happy.

After the breakup, Megan searched me out in the hallway between classes. She presented a worn envelope that contained a thin letter. The paper was edged with purple flowers.

"I wrote you every week." With that she turned and walked away. The letter was dated September 1 of our sophomore year.

"I'll be seeing you in all the old familiar places, that this heart of mine embraces all day through. In that small café, the park across the way, the carousel, the wishing well. I'll be looking at the moon, but I'll be seeing you."

Letters

One day, as I listened to my daughter plead for a cookie, my wife thrust a non-descript package into my hands. The manila envelope opened to yet another aged white envelope inside. That capsule was littered with doodles and etchings, some in the shapes of stars and hearts. Others were much vaguer, shapes without spines. The envelope had no name or return address; the front held only my name but no mailing address to find me. Curious, I gently opened it and unfolded the pages held within. They crinkled with age under my hands. Three pages in all, they were covered in large, girly script. More of the doodles and etchings filled the sides of the paper framing the words.

"I wonder if you wonder about me?" the note said, followed by other fragmented thoughts and lines.

"Sometimes I wish I was gone and not you; maybe you're the lucky one."

"I lay in bed and try not to be so dramatic. I know I am overreacting, but I can't seem to help the emotions. How is it I can be full of dread one minute and hope the next? Why is it that I am in love with you and moments later can't stand the thought of you?"

"Is it because you left me that I hate you so much? If I hate you, why do I keep lying in bed thinking of you?'

It was as if the scribe simply funneled the exact thoughts through her mind directly on to paper, with no thought about how they would sound in the cold light of day. It was a perplexing letter, and for the life of me I couldn't figure out who this letter was from and why she sent it. Could it be the same voice I had heard days before on the phone? These two oddities couldn't be a coincidence.

After a few days passed yet another letter showed up in a manila envelope. This letter held no doodles or etchings. Instead, the ink was pressed into the paper with great force. It stained the pores of the delicate paper with a dark, brooding blue ink. The letter raged against those that would force her into choices. Anyone of authority was held accountable. The author dismissed her parents with great malice. She found every fault and lifted them to the surface of the paper in condemnation. Every sour act she had committed could be drawn back to a choice her parents had made. It was the work of a self-inflicted victim, refusing to find any fault within herself.

The strange letters came nearly daily for ten days, fifteen letters in all, some rambling and filled with anger, while others held the fleeting fancy of a young girl in and out of love with the world around her. None held her name. After ten days, the strange packages stopped.

The only clue I could muster was that the post office they came from was only thirty miles north of my current home. Whoever was sending them was close. I pulled at the threads of my mind trying to figure out the meaning of all of this. I even wondered if this was a threat in some way to my family. I concluded likely not, but even so I called Mike and asked if he had any recollection of the mental picture of the girl in the letters. He struggled with an answer as the bulk of the girls he had spent time with were emotionally unstable, which was, of course, by design.

In a few days I forgot about the letters only to be abruptly reminded of the threat weeks later.

My Eighteenth Birthday

It was senior year and football was in full swing. The history of football at Prep was long and filled to the brim with success. During the 80's, Prep only lost ten games in the entire decade. They took home several state titles and sent many players to the college ranks and some on to the NFL. In fact, both of my cousins were star players during the 80's and went on to play for Bill Walsh at Stanford. I idolized them both, and as a kid I would play for hours in my yard pretending I was like them, a star Prep football player. Both Dinny and Jeff were over 6'7" and athletic. Both were diligent in the gym at getting stronger and watched what they ate to maximize their athletic prowess. You can imagine what a disappointment I was to everybody when I arrived.

That senior year I was 5'8" and weighed in at 210 pounds or so. What I lacked in an athletic physique I more than made up for with unnatural amounts of body hair. I had sat for months watching hair growing in places that terrified me. I was thankful I didn't have eyes in the back of my head for fear of just how ghastly the back of my body must look with a thick mane of hair growing out of it. I shaved my shoulders but that was really an act of denial. My senior year I did my best to change into my football attire in a dark corner, so no one could see my uncanny impression of Teen Wolf.

After the third day of football practice our head coach, a legend – just ask him – called me into his office and asked me to take a seat.

"Son," he began, "The coaches and I have been talking it over and we think it's in your best interest if you just quit. You know, do something you can truly excel at like, boy, I don't know, giving blood or competitive eating." He let out a rancid breath. "We just want you to succeed."

"Coach you want me to quit, to give up?" I responded.

"Yes, did I not make that clear?" he asked.

"But Coach, I thought you always taught us not to give up and not to give in."

"Boy, that speech is really coming back to bite me in the ass." He took a deep breath.

"Sometimes there are very special people who are made to quit, who are, in fact, at their best when they quit and really make everyone else better by just giving up, like the French for example. You are one of these people. The best thing you can do for the team is to turn in your pads."

"But Coach, all my life I wanted to play football at Prep. I wanted to play under the lights on Friday nights. I've had dreams about the fans chanting my name and visions of winning a state title with my teammates. This is who I am. This is what I want. You think I should just give that up?" I was pleading now, my voice strained and choked with phantom sobs.

"That's a pretty inspiring story, son. It reminds me of a boy I once knew. He, like you, wanted nothing more than to excel on the gridiron. He, like you, was born an unathletic, funny-looking boy. The coaches encouraged him to just give up, to give in and try to find a calling more suited to his skills. He defied them and stayed with the team and in time his hard work truly impressed the coaches, and even though he didn't play he won their respect." He slammed a wrinkled closed fist on his battered desk to drive home the point. This was Coach at his motivating best, pulling on thirty years of experience in getting the best out of young men and thrusting that knowledge at me.

"Coach, was that player you?" I asked in awe.

"Me? No, I was an all-state linebacker. That player was Ted Bundy. Is that what you want to be when you grow up? A monster, a serial killer? Because if you keep up with this idea of not quitting and staying on the team, I am afraid you will be on that path." He looked me fiercely in the eye.

"That path son, leads straight to the electric chair."

I buried my head in shame. This notion of quitting hit me like a two by four.

"I guess I see your point Coach. But it just feels wrong. I think I need to think about it."

"Good. Think about what I have said. I care about you and just want what's best. Hey, I hope I don't see you on the field today. Or ever again, really."

"Thanks Coach," I said as I walked out of his office.

I sought out Dan's advice on the matter. Dan was the star wide receiver now and one of the most popular kids in school – not because he was a great wide receiver but because he and his girlfriend would have sex in the back of his Ford Bronco at lunch and he would let some of us watch.

Dan was adamant that I keep playing. "You're like our mascot," he said. "I'll be damned if I am going to let them take our mascot. We need you to play."

"By mascot Dan, do you mean I am a leader?"

"Not really, I mean people follow you, but it's more out of morbid curiosity than leadership."

I had delusions of adequacy, and I wasn't going to let any coach take that away from me. I wouldn't quit.

As punishment for seeing me again, Coach made me the cord boy. What this meant was that when Coach put on his headset, I would follow him around holding his headset cord and keeping it from being tangled. This job was always reserved for a sophomore – not just any sophomore, but the sophomore who was the least likely to play – ever. The year before the cord boy had been Dan Holbert, who had recovered from severe polio as a child.

When I was handed that headset cord it was confirmation that I would never play my senior year. It wasn't just the fact that I wasn't a great football player that had me trailing our head coach around with his leash, it was the fact that I had disobeyed. The rules were clear and strict: You needed to workout with the team in the summer and attend camp. I was sent to live with my dad that summer, and he had moved 250 miles away. It wasn't possible to get back. Football would be another casualty of their divorce and the ongoing, bitter battle between my parents. I had played well my junior year and thought I might have really had a chance to contribute that final season. As I held that cord I decided that if this was the best way that Coach saw that I could contribute, then I would be the best cord boy in the league.

The season was rolling right along when my birthday came up – my eighteenth. The stripper birthday. We had a game against Wilson that Friday night and after that Dan, Mike, Andrew, and F-ing Walsh had all promised to take me out.

As the game rolled along I fastened and unfastened that cord like I had never done before. When Coach moved, I was right there to let out slack so he could roam that sideline unencumbered. When slack presented in the line I was quick to tighten it so no tripping mishap could be had. I was in the zone. If I had an A game, this was it.

We quickly ran the score up on Wilson. Tyson Thacker, our all-league running back, was well into the 200-yard mark by the time the gun sounded to end the third quarter. Our lead was up to thirty points and all that was left was to unload the bench and let some of the other seniors play. I watched one by one as my classmates poured on to the field. The clock ran, and I tried my best not to get excited about the hope that maybe I could get a few reps. On the other hand, who would man the cord?

I looked to the stands and saw my Dad sitting quietly on his hands, watching the game action. He had made the trip over to see me on my birthday. I hoped I could get in a few plays to make his journey worthwhile.

The minutes started to click away as the bench emptied. We led by a healthy 40-point margin now, but the Coach made no move to put me in. Above the din of the crowd I heard someone yell, "Come on, it's his birthday!"

"Yeah, let the fat one play! No, the other fat one. Not that one, the short hairy fat one, yeah that one. Let him play." Even with my mother's pleading he didn't make a move to put me in.

Then it came from the student section, a slow moving chant, gathering steam like a locomotive. Soon, the entire side of the stadium was chanting "Rudy! "as in Rudy Ruettinger, from Notre Dame, the miserable runt that inspired a movie and loads of misshapen twits to stick it out and never give up. Coach must hate that movie.

"Rudy, Rudy, Rudy!"

It took me a minute to realize they meant me. I certainly didn't see myself as a Rudy.

Coach Lock went over to the head coach and pleaded to let me in the game. He was losing the argument. Time was ticking away. Just over a minute left in the game when *finally*, Mr. Lock grabbed the back of my jersey and thrust me on the field. I tripped on my cord (irony?) and then righted myself and ran to the huddle. The crowd roared. On my first play as a nose guard, a position I had never played, I lurched forward and hit the center. My right arm fluttered down and then arced back as I hit him in the stomach as hard as I could. He gasped for air, and I discarded him and made a beeline to the QB. He slipped, and I tripped and landed on top of him. It was counted as a sack.

I played three plays before the game ended, and it was the best birthday gift I could have ever imagined. The crowd stormed the field and greeted me with high-fives and slaps on the back. Jason Francis, our all-world defensive end, picked me up in a giant bear hug of congratulations. It was the best night of my young life, and somewhere high above the field my old man took it all in.

After the game, I waited to shower so no one would see me naked and confuse me with the missing link, and then walked quietly to the parking lot. When I got there many of my teammates were still around, as were Mike, Andrew, and F-ing Walsh. Krissy held a "Happy Birthday" sign and Laura and Katie had a cake. The large ensemble sang "Happy Birthday" to me.

It was Krissy who had put it together. She had gathered the people up and purchased a large cake and a card for everyone to sign. She lingered back as people started to leave. Soon it was just her and me with her brother looming nearby.

"Happy birthday. You were awesome today."

"Were you at the game?"

"Well, yeah. I mean, I didn't see you play because I blinked, but you looked good with the cord. Anyhow, happy birthday."

With that, she gave me a hug.

"Did you do this? Put it together?"

"Sort of."

"Why?"

She shrugged her shoulders.

"First day of school last year I was all by myself at lunch. No one wanted to sit by me or had even really talked to me all day. You came by and sat with me for a few minutes just to say "hi." People like you and you stopped just to say hello. I just...I wanted to do something nice."

"Well thanks."

Mike pulled me away and scolded Krissy for interrupting our stripper time.

With that, Mike, Andrew, Dan, and F-ing Walsh joined me in Dan's soiled Ford Bronco and departed. Our first stop was Miss Kitty's, a dilapidated old building that functioned as a low-class strip club. We were low class people, so it seemed to fit. After working the nerve to go in - it took 25 minutes of each of us calling the other a pussy while we sat in the car - our gangly group of misfits entered the club. A misshapen, sad sack of a middle-aged men flipped through the *Wall Street Journal* behind a counter that had all sorts of sex toys in bright colors behind him. He chewed on a toothpick.

"Help ya?" he asked.

"Girls…girls," Andrew responded longingly.

We couldn't help but notice the tan thin waif on the small stage behind the oddly shaped man's shoulder. It slapped us silent.

"Hey fellas, you all eighteen?" asked Quasimodo.

"It's my birthday," I claimed loudly.

"Great. How about the rest of you?"

"Not all of us," said Mike, "but we make up for it with a strong desire to see these girls naked."

"Sorry fellas, gotta be eighteen."

As he said this the thin waif walked into the lobby, wearing a very small supply of clothing.

"Come on Jim; take it easy on the boys. They just want to have a good time."

"Rules is rules. You gotta be eighteen. Sorry boys, get a going where you're going."

Dejected, we walked out of Miss Kittie's. Not knowing what else to do, we just sat in the car plotting our next move. That was when we heard a soft knock on the window. It was the waif-thin stripper. We were all ashamed. Here we were degrading women at strip clubs, making them objects with our eyes, and this poor stripper was out here to lecture us. I am sure she was in law school, just trying to make a few dollars to help offset the enormous cost of tuition. My guess is that her poor daughter, whom she cared for by herself because the bastard father was out gallivanting on the town, was quietly waiting for her at home to tuck her in.

I lifted my arm heavy with shame to roll down the window.

"Hi guys, sorry about getting kicked out; that sucks. You're just looking for a good time. I think it's stupid that you have to be eighteen."

"Thanks," we muttered.

"I thought maybe you guys would want to see me naked."

Our ears perked up. Go on.

"Well, golly, I suppose we would," said Mike.

"It's my birthday,." my distant voiced echoed.

"How much?" asked Dan from the back. He'd had sex before, so he knew what women wanted.

"How much you got?"

I rolled up the window to confer. All told, after we had pulled change out of Andrew's mom's car, was $9.85 and a half pack of mint Chiclets.

I rolled down the window and Dan took over negations. "We have $9.85."

"And some Chiclets," added F-ing Walsh.

"Right, and some mint Chiclets."

"Ten bucks? That's it?"

"Yup."

"It's my birthday," I reminded her (in case she had forgotten the gravity of the situation).

"And some Chiclets."

"Fine," she said. "Pull around the back of the building. I'll meet you there in a minute."

Naturally, we did as we were told. A few minutes later the back door opened and out walked our waif. She was dressed in only a flimsy white sheet. An interesting choice, as it was about thirty-eight degrees out. We emptied out of the car and circled around our stripper. She was maybe twenty years old. She had ratty, curly red hair and teeth that leaned out over her chin like a horse. She was not an attractive woman, but we didn't care because she was going to be naked. At first, she simply opened her sheet and flashed us quickly. This drew the ire of Mike.

"No, no, no, we need to see something. Let us get a good look at you."

"Fine," she said.

After a few heart pounding moments (for us) she wrapped herself back up and took the money from Dan.

"And the Chiclets?" she asked, tapping her foot impatiently.

"Give her the gum, Walsh."

He groaned as he handed the packet to her. With that she bounded up the stairs and out of our lives forever.

The next morning, Saturday, I was filled with excitement. I had played football the night before and had a great birthday. Dan picked me up and we went back to school for our 9:00 A.M. meeting and films. Finally, I would be able to see myself play.

"How was last night?" he asked when I got in the car.

"Unbelievable. I had such a strong feeling. I can't believe just how excited I was. Is there anything better than that?"

"It was fun, but she was just a stripper."

"No, not the stripper, the game. I got to play."

As I walked into school Jason grabbed me.
"Hey buddy, how was last night?" he asked with a sly grin.

"Awesome. Words can't describe what I was feeling. Wow, what a rush. Sad to think it might never happen again."

"Oh, come on man, I am sure some girl will let you see her naked eventually."

"What? No man, I'm talking about the game," I said, irritated.

Mr. Lock joined in as well.

"Great night last night, huh? Hell of a birthday."

"Mr. Lock, I'm sorry, but it was just a nasty stripper who took ten bucks – no not even, $9.85 – to let us look at her naked for two seconds. It's not a big deal. I don't know why everyone cares."

"Well that's a good story, but I was talking about the game last night."

"Oh," I said into the ground.

"After films, you owe me laps."

"How many?"

"As many as it takes to get you right with God."

A month later my Dad returned to see me. It was our final football banquet. The awards got going and it was great to see my friends win.

Dan was the offensive MVP and Jason the defensive. Tyson won the Iron Man award for his hard work and toughness. Then the final award was presented.

"I would like to call up the team captains to help present this award," our head coach began.

"This final award is the only award voted on by the players themselves, so I am going to turn it over to Jason."

"This award goes to the most inspirational player on our team, the player who was always the last to talk to us before we took the field and the first to cheer a win or pick us up on a loss. He worked hard even though it was very unlikely he would play. He made us better players every day. He made us tougher. I don't need to say his name everyone knows who it is." Jason locked his eyes on mine. "Come on up."

With that, Dan pushed me forward. The room stood and applauded. It was the first and last time that I was truly speechless being recognized by these teammates whom I loved so much. That is the power of sports, to humble and inspire. As a football player, I liked to talk. I didn't think anyone really listened. My eyes were wet with gratitude. I mattered. Maybe not like my cousins, but I made a difference for our team. As the applause continued my father came up to hug me and was greeted by Mr. Lock.

"I am awfully proud of your son," he said to my father. "He inspires us every day."

"I know. He's a special kid," Dad responded.

Mr. Lock and I embraced in thanks for his mentorship. Both he and Dad had tears of pride in their eyes. I started to cry, too.

It was hard to believe I was never going to see that stripper again.

The Prom

My prom date was a girl named Becca. She had a certain reputation as a girl who got around. After I called her on the phone to ask her out, I came down with an ear infection. Becca was pretty in an Irish sort of way. She had sweeping red hair with green eyes and fair, freckled features. She was lean and loved to wear shirts that would rise to show her toned midriff. She had a full smile that showed her teeth and gums. Her voice was smoky and sultry, and she seemed to ooze sexual tension. That was good because when it came to sex I was at the very least tense. Not only was she sexy, but she was also dumb. She brought more weight to her bra then she did to the classroom. She was the head cheerleader, which I had hoped was a title she lived up to, and therefore was present at my glorious redemption on the football field that fall. Still, Becca was not convinced that she wanted me as a date for the prom.

"So, I was wondering if you...I mean if no one else has asked...I mean, would you like to go to the prom? I mean with me? I would be around. I would understand if you didn't want to tell anyone I was your date. I could just drop you off and maybe pick you up after."

"What are you talking about?"

"Do you want to go to prom with me?"

I could hear her eyes roll.

"Not really. I mean I was hoping anyone else would ask. If no one else asks, I guess I will go with you." She continued, "I will go only if there isn't another option. I will go with you only because being with you is less difficult to stomach than being sober for an entire evening."

"Wow, great. Perfect. I will pick you up at six."

"If no one else asks."

"Right. I am your last resort."

"Exactly."

"I wish I could tell you that this was the first time I had a date because someone said, 'Oh, what the hell it's better than staying home, clipping my toe nails.'"

"Whatever, just try to get some pot. I won't want to remember this."

Becca was a bit of a coup for me. For one, I was still feeling a disconnect with the ladies. I had gone from class clown who nobody wanted to touch to mysterious non-athlete who no one wanted to touch. Second, Becca was a popular score. She had broken up with Christian the QB just a week before and was not expected to be on the market. Everyone knew she was a party girl who when the pump was primed well was willing to have her pump primed. Christian and Becca had been dating since the start of the football season. It made perfect sense to Becca. She was, after all, the head cheerleader and Christian was the star. On the other hand, Becca was a shallow slut, who if she had a thought in her head it would surely perish from loneliness, and Christian was a douche bag. He spent more time asking how he looked in his football uniform than he did deciphering the playbook. Plus, they were both gingers, and two wrongs don't make a right. The last thing we need is more red heads running around, with their flaming orange hair, translucent skin and visible blue veins.

As the week wore down, it was becoming more and more evident that no one else was going to ask Becca to prom. This may have been due to the fact that I openly challenged any man to a fistfight if they would ask her. No one can prove that was the definitive reason. As part of her outreach to not make prom the worst day of her life, Becca decided to invite me over to help her make cookies for the baseball team. She envisioned me helping her to create the perfect dessert and taking the warm treats and packing them in carefully decorated brown bags while I envisioned her topless. We were both disappointed. The first batch of cookies came out of the oven bubbling with sugary goodness. She let them cool while we sipped on lemonades that she had spiked with vodka. When the adequate time had passed, Becca attempted to scoop them off the cookie sheet only to find them stuck. She torqued her elbow back to provide maximum leverage and strength only to find the wafers incapable of moving. I did my best to help, but only managed chipping the cookies apart with a chisel and hammer.

"What the hell did you do to these things?"

"Nothing," she said. "I followed the directions. How hard are cookies supposed to be?"

"Well, these ones feel hard as granite."

"I mean, how dumb do you have to be to screw up cookies?"

"Well Becca, that's what we are trying to ascertain."

"Ascertain?"

She sounded out the word slowly with her mouth. What a waste of a mouth.

"Never mind. Did you grease the bottom of the pan?"

"Of course. I put Crisco all over the bottom."

"Did you put the Crisco on the spot the cookies now rest, or did you put it on the actual bottom?"

"Ohhhhh."

With that she took another long sip of her vodka lemonade.

"It's a good thing you're beautiful."

"You think I am beautiful?"

"Of course, I wouldn't chip apart an ugly girl's cookies," I said, banging the sheet against the brick fireplace.

With that, she formed a self-conscious smile that played on the edges of her lips, and we had our first moment. We finished the cookies, taking more care this time, and started to make bags. As I moved around the small kitchen I used any excuse I could find to brush up against her body, to sweep her hair, and to breathe in the vanilla perfume she wore. I soaked in the image of her in her tight jeans and simple white t-shirt.

She was striking. I, on the other hand, was a replacement. I was not meant to be her date, Christian was. She had spent the better part of six months dreaming of going to prom with the QB. She had picked out what dress she would wear, had bought the perfect shoes, and had planned the day of makeup and prep work with her "besties." She had the after-party planned and even what undergarments she would remove as she offered herself up to him. She would have been disappointed with Christian; if football had taught me anything it was that he had a quick release under pressure. I was a poor substitute for Christian, but as she was licking dough off a battered wooden spoon she was eyeing me. Maybe, just maybe, I would do the trick.

After consulting Krissy on the matter, I was told I needed to make a bigger romantic move to seal a positive evening with Becca. In hindsight, Krissy may have been doling out bad advice. It wouldn't be a stretch considering all the terrible advice her incompetent brother had given me over the years. Krissy and I had found a soothing habit. Three or four times a week she and I would meet on the bluff near my house to smoke cigarettes and gossip. The view was always nice, and a few benches provided a nice seat. I didn't really smoke, but it was nice to find time with Krissy to discuss my many female-inspired insecurities and gauge her opinion. Krissy was adamant that I write Becca a song on the piano and sing it to her. She may have been fucking with me.

I started to pen a song just for Becca. I spent a few hours at the piano putting the whole package together on a Friday night. Of course, I had the time to do this because nobody had invited me out to do anything. I normally would have gone to bed, but my mother had made me promise to be her designated driver and pick her up at the Taproom when the bar closed.

I wrapped up my simple opus, "Shades of the Soul," and called Krissy to tell her.

"I am coming over, I want to hear it." There was a charge of electricity in her voice.

"I guess, but it's a little embarrassing."

"I will be the judge of that."

A few minutes later Krissy arrived on foot. Her blond hair was whipped up above her head and her soft features washed out in the harsh light of the naked bulb on the porch. She was shivering, as she had not worn a coat, just a thin sweatshirt and some jeans. I put my arms to her shoulders and rubbed them to get blood flow.

"Cold," she shivered.

I made a cup of hot chocolate and brought it into the music room. There the baby grand sat, quietly holding the stories of my hours of emotional wreckage I had buried into it. Krissy took a seat on the couch and waited.

"I mean, it may not be that good. If it's not just let me know and I can try something else."

"Just play it."

I started with the opening chord: C-minor.

"I mean maybe this is too much; she might think it's too weird."

"Just play it."

"I am just saying maybe a nice Hallmark card could do the trick."

"Play the fucking song before I bash this ceramic mug over your head."

Terrified to face her wrath, I started playing in earnest. "Shades of the Soul" was possibly the worst song ever written. Laughable for many reasons, one being the fact that I sang rhymes such as "love" with "leather glove" and "heartache" with "clam bake." Sappy and intense, it was as creepy as any song a serial killer would write for someone. When I stopped singing, Krissy did the unthinkable: she applauded in a sign of support.

"Wow. Play me more."

She sat and listened for what must have been an hour as I ran my fingers over the keys, flexing the strings of the piano. She quietly watched as I became more and more engrossed in the sound, and she started to fade to the background. At last I was done.

I sat hunched for a moment lost, forgetting she was there.

"You're really good. Will you play for me again sometime?"

"Sure," I answered, "just let me know when."

"Okay record that song on a tape for Becca. Give it to me and I will put it into her gym bag during PE. We have the same class."

"I am thinking of making a mix tape, you know, add some other romantic favorites."

She rolled her eyes.

"Whatever, just give it to me on Monday. That will give you a week to build on before the prom."

In addition to my classic, "Shades of the Soul," I added a Barry Manilow favorite called "I need You Now," a truly stalker-like jingle that assured a certain freak-out factor from the recipient. I wrote a little note that only made me sound more desperate and possibly dangerous and gave the package to Krissy. She did as she said and delivered the tape to Becca. What I would learn later is that my masterpiece never made it to her. Instead Krissy took the liberty of making a tape with a lone song, "I Wanna Hold Your Hand." Becca thought it was the cutest thing ever and, more importantly, so did all her friends.

Prom night started off on the wrong foot when I found out I was not allowed to use the car. I had no money and therefore no car of my own and was left to the whims of my mother for transportation. With no car to use I had only my '84 Schwinn. I figured Becca had little desire to ride the handle bars that night. If she was going to ride anything I hoped it wouldn't be handle bars. I was stuck. I called Sam. Sam was a linebacker on the football team and one of the few friends who returned my calls. He also preferred the big girls and had not asked anyone to prom for fear of being found out as a bovine lover. I asked to borrow his car, and being the sport that he was he gladly complied. The problem was that his truck was massive. He had special tires that made the truck rise a healthy five feet from the ground. I needed to stand on his shoulders just to climb in the cab. I had no idea how I was going to get Becca into the truck.

"That's the beauty of it, you have to prop the ladies on your shoulders to get them in the car. It's like automatic first base."

"Sam, with the heifers you date, I'm surprised you haven't thrown out your back."

"I did, Tabitha last weekend; I'm seeing the chiropractor on Thursday."

"Sam, what should I do with the three rifles on the gun rack?"

"It's prom, I thought you should use protection."

"I am pretty sure this isn't the protection I am supposed to use."

I got nothing but a blank stare back from Sam.

"What kind of protection do you mean?" asked Sam at last.

"A condom…to put on your penis during sex."

"Why would you put something over your penis? Do you put a rain slicker on a grizzly bear? You must let the king snake be free."

"I wouldn't know."

"Well with this truck your chances have doubled at least. This truck is better than a roofie. Well, it could also be because the carbon monoxide is leaking into the cab, you may want to crack a window. Or if you need a little assistance hold your breath for a few minutes and watch the lady slink to the floor, either way."

"Thanks Sam."

"No problem. If things go well for you just hose out the cab. Had Tabitha in there just last night; when we're together our sex smells like chocolate syrup."

"That might be the most disgusting thing I have ever heard."

Sam just grinned at me, proud of his conquest.

I rolled the lumbering truck beast through the streets, trying to not crush any stray Hondas that might have approached as I drove toward Becca's house. I figured the rifles would come in handy if I got any shit from Becca's dad. Rumor had it he liked to pull the old "I will be up cleaning my gun when you get home" routine. When he opened the door to greet me I had Sam's 12-gauge shotgun on my shoulder.

"Good evening, sir," I began, "is Becca home? I am taking her to prom."

I cocked the rifle.

"Is that a gun?"

"Yes, sir, 12-gauge. Thought I might get in little cleaning tonight before I dropped her off. Is that going to be a problem?"

"Nope, none at all. I have a little .22 rifle I keep by the door."

"That sounds adorable. You kill a lot of squirrels with that thing?"

"Screw it," he said, walking away from the door. "Becca, you're...date... is here."

"Bye, Daddy," Becca said as she kissed her father. "I will be home when I feel like it," and burst out the door.

She took one look at the truck and then noticed the 12-gauge.

"The truck came with the rifle."

"Couldn't get a limo?"

"I am lucky I got a tux. For a while I thought I was going to have to wear black trash bags cut to look like a one. I don't have much money. Come on, climb on my shoulders so you can get in."

Becca straddled my shoulders, awkwardly trying to get into the cab. In case you were wondering, it smelled nothing like chocolate syrup.

She wore an elegant black dress that fell to her ankles. She had matching evening gloves that rode up her arm to her elbow. She had her deep red hair pulled back except for two strands which loosely framed either side of her face. She wore a tight necklace with silver and embedded dark jewels and matching earrings that dangled from her lobes. Her neckline plunged but revealed nothing, damn it.

"You look tired," I said.

"Thanks."

"I mean you look beautiful; you just seem tired."

"I am a little hung over; there was lot of drinking and partying last night. What did you do?"

"I sat at home mostly, I had to pick my mother up from the bar. I played the piano for a while."

"Wow, you are such a virgin."

"I don't think that's such a bad thing."

"That's what all the virgins say." She rolled her eyes at me as she said this.

"Hey, listen, can we stop at my friend's house before the dance? I want to show her my dress."

"Sure thing."

Becca implored me to stay in the truck while she ran into her friends. After thirty minutes, she had yet to return to her chariot, so I carefully climbed down from the truck, trying not to twist an ankle on the way down. After knocking on the door a few times, a small blond girl I recognized from school came to the door. She was dressed in sweats.

"Becca fell asleep about 20 minutes ago."

"She did?"

"Yeah, she had a lot of vodka last night."

"I heard that. Well, just tell her thanks for the night. She can call me tomorrow if she wants."

"You're just going to leave?"

"Sure. A good night's sleep is important."

"Jesus. You are some kind of pussy. She told me you were like silly putty; I thought she meant you were just fat. I'll go wake her."

Once Becca was fully awake, we went to the dance. She and I spent most of the night complaining about our exes. Or her ex on her side and my "never-had-her" in Megan and "failed-to-have-her" in Angela. She had been pretty broken up about Christian, but was excited to move on. I guess she had moved on with three different guys in three days. She was recovering nicely. Still, she didn't know how long it would take to get over him. I subtly encouraged her to continue on her current therapeutic path, hoping to be a fourth statistic. As the night wore on she dropped her barriers and basic disgust of me. As we headed to the after-prom party she had chosen, she turned to me and said, "Thanks for tonight. It turned out to be pretty fun. I thought seeing Christian with another girl would kill me, but talking to you about it...I don't know, it just seemed to hurt less. You're a great listener."

"Thanks."

"I'm getting lightheaded."

"Oh right, roll down the window."

At the party, just three couples arrived at an empty house. All Becca's friends giggled and danced while chugging beers. I was proud to say that my date could out beer-bong everyone in the room. She was certainly a lady, I thought, as a large belch escaped her lips.

It was nearing 2:00 A.M. when a drunken Katie stumbled up to me as I watched the party from the couch.

"Doesn't Becca look pretty tonight?"

"Of course. She is beautiful. She always has been."

"Don't you want to dance with her?"

"Yeah, but she made it pretty clear that she isn't really into me. She seems pretty broken up about Christian."

"Help her forget Christian. Dance with her."

Katie stumbled over to Becca, who was gyrating to the beat of the music, or at least as best as she could, what with the alcohol poisoning starting to take hold.

"Your date is so sweet, Becca."

"Yeah, he is."

"That tape he gave you was the cutest thing ever."

"You think so?"

"Yes, I am soooo jealous. Why don't you go over there and give him one of your famous dances?"

"You're really jealous?"

"Yes, we all are. We would be even more jealous if you two hooked up."

"Well, then – watch this."

With that Becca walked over to me at the couch and held her hand out to be taken.

"Come dance with me."

The music pumped out a loud beat as we struggled to catch the wave of the rhythm. Becca started with her arms around my shoulders and her hips shaking side to side, but as the song gathered steam so did she. Soon her arms were wrapped around my neck, and I could feel her breasts crushed up against my chest. Her hips still swayed side to side but now in a much closer proximity to my own. Something told me that her Dad would not appreciate this.

I looked deep into her emerald eyes. "Wow," I said, feeling my "king snake" take notice of the situation. Can I call it that?

"I loved that tape you gave me. It was so sweet."

"Golly, thanks," I said, exhaling heavily in her face. I had forgotten to breathe.

With that she planted her lips on mine. It took a second to find the match, but then we fit our lips together. As she pulled away she bit softly into my lower lip, pulling it.

"Let's go downstairs and dance in private. Did you bring protection?"

"I still have the 12-gauge."

"I meant a condom."

"I think I have some Saran wrap."

"You're so cute."

"Aren't I though."

A knock came at the door. It was quiet at first then it became a rapid pounding.

Becca looked out the window.

"Oh, shit, it's Christian. Don't let him in."

He called my name to let him in. Dumbfounded, I stood in front of the door.

"Come on, let's just go downstairs," Becca pleaded.

Christian responded, "Come on, man, we're teammates."

I looked over at Becca, my eyes wet with tears. Why was he doing this?

I opened the door. Christian burst in.

"Becca, come on. Can we talk? To see you with another guy – I guess we can call him that – is driving me crazy."

"No talking, Christian. I'm moving on."

Christian turned to me. "Come on, tell her I just want to talk."

"What happened to your date?"

"Oh, she wanted nothing to do with me. How do I look by the way? I think this tux is really working for me."

"Becca, he seems pretty beat up, maybe you should talk?" I reasoned.

"What the hell is wrong with you?" Katie shouted at me.

"I don't know," I said flustered, "I just don't want to stand in the way of love. I mean, maybe they are meant to be together."

"Are you kidding me?" Katie responded. "Choir guys."

Becca and Christian disappeared downstairs, the downstairs that Becca and I could have been in. After ten minutes Christian came rushing up and pulled me aside.

"Listen, as you know, Becca and I have been through a lot, and we really need to work on some things. She's hoping it would be okay if I took her home. I said as my friend and teammate I am sure you would be fine with it."

"I guess, Christian, if that's what she really wants."

"Great," he said, patting me on the back.

When he descended the stairs, he ran into Becca who was coming up the stairs to see me. He grabbed her and told her that I was leaving, that my mother had called me demanding I return home because I was late for curfew.

"He asked me to take you home."

Becca's shoulders slumped. "If that's what he really wants." She looked past Christian and saw me putting my coat on. She came up to me and looked me in the eyes and left a soft kiss on my lips.

"Bye."

"I will call you in the morning to see that you got home alright." With that I walked out the door with my eyes buried on my shoes.

The next night I met Krissy on the bluff. She wanted a full report. When I told her she took the back of her hand and swung it. It connected at the base of my shoulder.

"I can't believe you screwed this up. Everyone put in so much work for you. Man, you couldn't get laid in a whore house."

"Well that hardly seems fair. I don't want to be the one who steps in between two people who might fall in love."

"Love," she said. "You know what love is? It's when we find someone whose oddness and eccentricities are compatible with our own set of fears and emotional stiltedness and we fall into a mutually deep and satisfying comfort. We call this love. Oh, well. Becca has fat armpits."

The Second Call

It had been several days since I received the tattered and worn package of letters in the mail and had two weeks since that first phone call, when the phone hummed once again past the witching hour. I picked up the receiver. Both my wife and daughter were secure in the depths of their slumber and went undisturbed.

"Hello?" I whispered into the phone.

A heartbeat passed and then I heard my name. The caller was speaking to me in a cooing style that could only be one phantom from the past. Whenever a late-night phone call comes in, your heart sinks. It could be a disaster waiting on the other end. Your mind tends to rumble away from you towards all the possible, awful possibilities about what could have gone wrong. My heart was still lodged in my throat as the realization set in as to who was on the other line. I could see her in my mind, her hair gently being tugged as she nervously wrapped it in her fingers, her body curled up against a wall as she rested while talking to me. I could see her, and I am sure that through the magic of our universe, she could see me.

"I am all alone," she said quietly, just above a whisper.

"Why?"

"I have to be if I'm going to get any better. If I'm going to be able to make it. I have to be alone."

"No one is all alone."

"I am. I've discarded anyone who ever loved me or tried to love me."

175

"Why would you do that?"

"They didn't matter as much to me as my lifestyle did. I sent them away, and now they won't come back."

"How do you know that?" I asked. "Surely those who truly love you will always love you."

"I thought that, too, for a while. I figured, 'Hey, these are my friends, boyfriends, parents, siblings – they will always be here in my corner. I can steal their money or their TV, but when push comes to shove they'll be there.' I guess at some point they had to throw in the towel. I mean how many flat screens can you have stolen by someone until you stop inviting them into your home?"

"Depends. How big were the flat screens? Maybe two?"

She chuckled a little and then was lost for a moment in her own scorched memories.

"I've always been beautiful, or at least I think people thought I was beautiful. You know what I have learned since I have been here?"

"No, what's that?" I softly replied.

"I've learned that I'm ugly. For all the work I have done on my body, my soul is ugly. I don't even know what beauty is anymore. I can't see it in the mirror, I can't see it in others, and I can't see it anywhere. The world just seems so dark to me sometimes."

"That depends on how you chose to view the world. Sure, there are prisms though which you can view facts that make everything seem worse than it really is. Or you can choose to view the world as it could be, to believe in yourself, in others. You'll find that when you seek out a little hope the world isn't nearly so bleak."

"God, how do you believe that shit?"

"You're not the only one who owns the rights to personal demons."

"Yeah, but you sound like such a pussy."

In the darkness of my room I shrugged my shoulders. How many times in my life would I hear what a pussy I am? Well I wasn't the one making crazy phone calls in the middle of the night, so that had to count for something.

"At least you're somebody," she said quietly.

"You're somebody."

"I am nobody. You can't be alone and be somebody. Those who love you, think of you, and live for you make you. Me, I am nobody, just a shadow of someone who used to be somebody."

I could hear her voice get caught in her throat as the words sank into her very being. She believed them, and it hurt.

"You're right, though," she said. "Maybe someday I will be loved, able to feel love. I hope so."

I could see her freckled cheeks stained with tears quietly rolling down her face.

"I really want to feel something again, something other than guilt or shame. I was beautiful once."

I didn't know what to say, so I said nothing. The phone line was quiet as I listened to her breathing for a moment, and then I could hear her gently set the receiver back in its cradle and disconnect the call.

My breathing was jagged and my muscles were sore. I didn't realize how hard I was squeezing the phone. As my heartbeat found its usual rhythm again, I thought about being somebody. I looked over at my wife with her soft features and my daughter curled in her arms, and I realized it's true: I was nobody until them. All my life I wanted to be somebody, and I finally truly achieved it, but only when it was in their eyes.

Isn't that what everyone needs? To be somebody to someone who matters.

The Choir Tour

Towards the end of my senior year, we prepared for the annual choir tour. This was a four-day trip taken with the entire choir (40 or so students) to various churches and high schools around the region. This was to be the last of my high school choir life and it held a special significance to me. Mr. Lock had been like a father to me for my three years in his choir. Those years had so much anxiety, as well as curiosity, and he had been a gentle guide through all of it. He had nurtured my joy of music and taught me how to use it as a positive outlet. He had called me out on behavior that was unbecoming, and he had left me with the motivation to do well by him. In this final tour, I wanted to savor the music and his companionship. I also wanted to take the time to truly enjoy my friends. Our time was running out and soon enough we would go to the senior campout and then our own separate ways. We might stay in touch, but we all knew that it would never be the same.

This unique chapter of our life that is high school was drawing to a close, and I felt I had so much left undone (most of them women). Of course, there was also Megan. This would provide me one last chance to spend time with her. She and I had found a comfortable level of discourse: she would walk into the classroom, I would stare. The end.

Her spirit was as fetching as ever, and I was still caught in her web. Every day I seemed to wrap myself up tighter and tighter. Sometimes when we would sing I would watch her – the way her chest contracted and expanded with the words, the shape of her mouth, and the twinkle in her eye as beautiful music poured out of her. It was as intoxicating to me as any drink. The feeling that came with observing her was not one of joy, but rather one of despair. She wasn't mine. I wanted more than anything to make her mine, but she kept eluding my grasp like a fleeting wind.

Sometimes she would walk into class and wrap her arms around me in a hug and look up into my eyes before leaving me with just the ghost of a smile. Other times she would sulk to her seat and wait for the relief and distance the music could bring her. Either way, I watched over her with that same ball of despair in my stomach. It all seemed so hopeless.

As we got on the bus to leave, I sat next to Christian. I didn't really like Christian, but we had gotten caught up in a discussion about Andrew and I wanted to finish it. Apparently, Andrew's girlfriend wanted to become a feminist, but he wouldn't let her.

Christian and I took the far back seat of the bus. This seat was actually a three-person bench, but we figured that no one would take the third seat, giving us access to extra space. To my utter surprise, Megan strode down the aisle and planted herself in between the two of us. We were tight enough that her thigh had to rub against mine, which (naturally) was just aces with me. She wore a pair of light colored jeans that were stylishly ripped to reveal parts of her upper leg and the back of her hamstring (not that I noticed). She wore a white t-shirt with a baby blue sweater with a plunging V-neck. The color of the sweater mirrored her eyes, making them shine.

I tingled; it's not very manly, but it's true. I didn't want the pressure and grave responsibility of sitting next to her. What if I fell asleep and farted? Would she believe it was Christian when I blamed it on him? Why was she sitting next to me in the first place?

It was early in the morning as the bus departed. We had a four-hour drive ahead of us before our first stop. Megan placed a set of headphones on her ears and rested her head on my shoulder. She looked up to give me a simple smile of thanks and fell asleep. The warmth of her body spread over me as I rested my head against the window and stared out at the passing scenery. I fell into a light sleep and dreamt about what could be.

The first concert on the tour took place in a small church with only a few dozen people in attendance. As per protocol, we dressed in our cheap used tuxes while the girls decked themselves in black dresses that reached the tops of their shoes. The tuxes had been purchased by the school from a funeral home and still had the subtle stench of embalming fluid. If you concentrated all the coats together one could get a pretty good buzz going, or at least so said one of the bassists, Cory Frazier.

The Prep choir was good, even very good, and the small crowd was appreciative of the treat they were in for. Two of the girls would go on to become professional opera singers and the aforementioned Cory Frazier would star in theater. One alto would go on to become a mildly successful jazz singer and tour on all the finest cruise lines. And of course, there was Megan. She was the best of all of them. It was not a question of if she could make it on a label, it was if she would choose to go for it. Fear seemed to hold her back.

While the choir weaved rocking secular music in with the more tepid religious harmonies, it allowed the dreamers to open their thoughts and drift. I don't know what the others thought when the music allowed the mind to free itself and soar, but for me the music pulled my dreams to the future. What was in store? Like so many, I was fearless. I had no doubt I would be fine. I didn't fear college or anything that life had to offer; I was a fighter, and I would fight through anything. Funny how the future holds so many unknowns, but youth disregard the fear and forged ahead into the dark unknown. But when it came to love, we were left quivering in terror.

I wanted so much to be in love and be loved in return – to feel the warm embrace of the peace that love gives us, the embrace I had never felt before. As I grew older, I can't recall just how many times I thought to myself that life would be perfect if I only had someone to share it with. Why does this fear take hold? Why are we so afraid of rejection? For me I knew I didn't have a lot to offer. I was short and chubby. I had far too much body hair for taste. I didn't have the washboard abs of the good looking popular guys, the ones that seemed to have all the girls, the Joe Gaukrogers of the world. Instead I had a decent sense of humor, even if it was somewhat offensive to women. I could play the piano and had a burning desire to be the hero in a story. I was not the type who wins the big game, but I was a steady rock of a guy. I felt like I could be the guy that all others could count on when the chips were down. If you needed help, if you needed to talk, I was the guy. I wouldn't hurt anyone. I was the gentle giant (minus the giant). I played this role well. Whenever a girl had a problem with a guy, I was there to lean on, to provide a shoulder and some unthreatening comfort. If the guy in question had a problem with it, I was willing to fight it out. This made me an island. A lot of guys didn't want anything to do with me and the girls found me to be the human equivalent of a blankie. I was okay with that because in my mind I thought I was doing the right thing.

My dad had always said, "Character is what you do when no one else is watching."

I held that at my core. I drove the drunk girls home; I pulled them away from the hormonally charged jackals who might have been circling. If the guys had problems with it, again, we would fight it out. I felt it was what women wanted deep down. If I wasn't going to get them to swoon when they looked at me, then the very least I could hope for was that they would grow up to realize that they missed the right guy and died miserable and broken wondering what if they had chosen the protector, the gentleman. Of course, I also hoped they would grow to become 290 pounds and repulsive to others so they would die alone while I spent my weekends on a tropical beach with my bikini model wife. I didn't think it was too much to ask.

Maybe some girls would grow up and look back and say that I was the kind of guy they needed and missed. Most likely they never gave it a second thought. It was sad just how many great relationships I had ruined because I was too afraid to tell them how I felt, to risk leaving that friendship zone and asking to be more. Now in my "old age" I realize just how much I missed out on because I was unable to lighten up, but unlike others I became a grown-up at a very early age. I didn't know how to relax, and I didn't know how to love without it being a suffocating affliction for the recipient. This is where my mind went during those songs. Or something like that.

I roomed with Jay, a fellow tenor and a good friend. Jay and I were cut from a similar cloth. We both liked musicals, but never came to an agreement on who was a better stage composer: Sondheim or Webber. For those of you who don't know who those people are, it's likely because instead of following musical theater you were out getting laid. I had the free time to ponder these issues. Besides that riveting debate, Jay and I would also spend several long-winded tactical conversations on how to win Megan, but I'll get to that in a moment.

As we took our seats on the bus to depart to our next concert, Megan boarded the bus late and ambled down the aisle.

Megan had a flare for the dramatic, so the fact that she was late was little surprise, and the fact that she was late because she had charmed a smoke out of the church deacon was even less of a surprise. What was a surprise was that rather than taking a seat between Christian and me, she planted her perfect bottom on my lap. She wrapped her arms around my neck, looked into my eyes, and then pulled her head back to laugh. Her hair whipped from one side to the other as she locked her gaze on…Christian.

What the hell was going on here? She hadn't been this close to me since seventh grade and Seven Minutes in Heaven. She stopped to rest her head on my shoulder like a child. I could feel her breath on my neck. Jay later told me I had the look of an inmate being sentenced to the hole for something he didn't do – just clueless. Christian was clueless, too, for as most of you female readers have likely already pieced together (but your male counterparts have yet to grasp) is that Megan had chosen me as a suitable pawn with which to tease Christian. Christian was the target of her lust, at least for the moment. At the time, all I could figure was that Megan had finally come to her senses and was professing her true love for me. Right.

I was growing bolder. Jay could sense it too. Sure, he knew how I felt about Megan, but most guys felt that way about her. I was starting to seek her out. I would sit next to her at dinner or look for her to wish her good luck prior to a concert. Her flirtations had emboldened me, something I am not sure that Megan was prepared for.

My courting style was similar to the death of Giles Corey: it was like rocks being placed one by one on your chest until it crushed you. Megan was now in for this treat. I was not alone in this quest; Christian was now on the playing field. Her game with me had certainly worked on him. After our second concert to a handful of the devoted, I pulled him aside to let him know that the game was on. I was going to fight him for her.

"I don't know what that means," I told Jay, "but we will come up with something."

Jay shook his head and had the same look the Christians had before fighting the lions.

On our final night, we sang to the only packed house to which we would perform. It was a seminary, a training ground for priests. The small chapel held only a hundred or so souls but featured high ceilings and marble floors, which made for beautiful acoustics. The virgin masses (I could relate) all filled in as we opened with a stunning arrangement by Franz Beibl of "Ave Maria."

The sound of the notes as they filled the church and wrapped about us was stunning. We felt as if we could reach out and take hold of the notes. The piece of music was riveting in its subtle chords, and it set a respectful, reflective tone. I would steal looks at Megan as she sang on the other side of the choir formation. Her eyes were closed as she unleashed the notes required, her mouth forming the Latin words. She could hear everything, and when it came time for her solo she launched into the simple few measures required without missing a beat before the choir once again powerfully backed her. She was at peace here. Her demons exorcised, she was able to just live and feel the power and beauty of the music. She was never more splendid to me than in that moment.

It wasn't until near the end of our concert that the idea occurred to me. We were singing a Robert Burns poem, "A Red, Red Rose."

Oh My Luve's like a red, red rose
That's newly sprung in June:
Ooh my Luve's like a melodie
That is sweetly play'd in tune!

As fair art thou, my bonnie lass,
So deep in luve am I:
And I will luve thee still, my dear,
Till a' the seas gang dry.

It struck me that I had nothing left to give Megan but the truth. I couldn't go on longing from afar; it hurt too much. And though it was better to have the hope that maybe, just maybe, she would see me the way I saw her than to have it crushed with her rejection, I wasn't about to let her close herself into a dark room with Christian while I was left with that "what if I told her" punishment. This would be the first of many times I would have this pep talk with myself, and the results would all, sadly, turn out the same. I blame it on my metabolism.

As we got to the final piece of our show, Mr. Lock's favorite piece, "Jesus Christ the Apple Tree," my mind was made up. I would write her a letter and give it to her on the bus as we left for home. By the time we landed at the school curb I would have the answer I had sought for six years. I would either start living or start dying. Can you believe a woman could have such power?

Back in my day, all we had were notes. Now people can text or email or Facebook. It's all the same, a way to say what you needed to say without the uncomfortable stare of your lusted-for target bearing down on you. People would pass notes from class to class expressing their true feelings under the protection of paper and space. It was cowardly, but it was also the most truthful way to give and receive information.

I watched the twitching hands of Mr. Lock as they sliced the air leading us, his choir, in a triumphant finish. He had such joy on his face. His short dark hair was moistened with sweat and his large round glasses reflected the lights. A smile crept on his lips and smoothed his brow as the music washed over him. Like Megan and me, here he found his solace in the world, his most perfect place.

What we didn't know at the time was that Jack Lock, my coach, my teacher, my mentor, and my friend, was only nine months from a cold silent grave. Even as he led us, a cancerous tumor was preparing to strike in his brain. He would fight, but it would be quick. He was forty-eight. He would leave a wife and a sixteen-year-old daughter, but he was also a father to many. His funeral would burst the seams of the cathedral. Years of students would be present to pay final respects. At the apex of the ceremony each student in attendance was asked to circle around the dark casket singing "Jesus Christ the Apple Tree." We all knew the words, even those from twenty years prior. It was a terrible performance wracked with the sobs of grief and the rustiness of time. He would have hated it.

So much time and energy goes into following those famous around us. Star athletes have 24-hour coverage and countless magazines cover Hollywood stars, but what brings us together are those who formed our lives. Mr. Lock was a guiding hand in creating the men and women he taught. He taught us love and respect for others and ourselves. He brought us together and made a family out of those who might have felt different or lost and alone. Not a week goes by – even now, twenty years later – that I don't think of him and feel sorry for myself. I wish he had been at my wedding and had been able to meet my wife. I wish he could meet my daughter and teach her to embrace music like he did me. I wish I could just seek his advice. No network covered him and those like him, no magazines wrote their stories. Instead, they toiled in relative poverty and the shadows of day-to-day life, yet they were the true heroes, and they got lost because we were too young to understand. Now, they are the voices in our heads.

But Mr. Lock isn't gone. He lives on through his students. His message has been shared with them and they have taken it into their careers and lives and passed it along. It isn't a message in words, but rather a way of life: Love! Love enough to discipline, love enough to listen, love enough to seek out those who need the shelter. Here he was, nine months before his death, in front of a packed house, his adopted children singing a beautiful song spreading that dedication to love to all in attendance. You could see the pride in his eyes. Soon those eyes would be subdued from the cancer, but that night they danced.

Towards the end, he was home in hospice care with his wife and daughter. He had some visitors from time to time, but most had said their piece, and he had so little energy that he spent as much time as he could with just his family. I received word that he was asking to see me. I would need to travel the five hours to see him, and I used my job and the distance as reason not to go. In reality, it was the fear of seeing him near death, his voice weak and his body a shell. I didn't want to see the man who had helped shape me in that state. He would have been tiny and frail, unable to speak for more than a few sentences before fading in and out. I didn't want to look at him like that while the music he loved soothingly played nearby. I wanted to see him as the inspiration he was. I wanted to see him in front of that chapel leading his choir in triumphant song. I was afraid to face him; I was afraid to let him down.

Instead I sat and wrote a tearful three-page letter (a pattern of mine, I know). I told him all I felt and thanked him for his kindness and belief in me when so few had any it was cathartic but also wrenching to write and say good-bye. A few days later he died, and I attended the funeral. When I returned to my college dorm after the funeral, the letter sat on my desk. It had been returned. In my haste, I forgot to add the zip code to the address. I never got to tell him. I hadn't made that mistake with Megan, maybe because the stakes weren't as high. I vowed to never let anything go unsaid again.

I spent the better part of that final night of the tour writing my feelings to Megan. When I got on the bus I sat in a new seat. I told myself that if she chose to sit by me I would give her the letter. She took a seat next to me forcing me out of the window seat and onto the aisle. That was the sign. I handed her the note.

"Just read this, I don't need you to say anything if you don't want to; you just need to know."

She read the entire letter. When she was done, she folded it up and put it in her pocket. She smiled and hugged me and then fell asleep with her head against the window. That was it.

When I got home it was already dark. I ate a quiet dinner with my mom and then adjourned to the music room to play the piano. I quietly played my sorrow away, feeling the release of the pain through the keys. My mother came in and sat and listened while drinking her wine. When I finished, I sat with my back hunched over, spent.

"Did I tell you about the time your father first asked me out?" my mother said.

"No, thanks. I don't need to be grossed out with feelings right now."

"He was eighteen and had just graduated from high school. He went to public school, and they got out a few days before we did. He lived next door, you know, and as soon as the ceremony was over he came to the door to ask to take me out that night."

"Yeah, what did you say?"

"I said 'no,' of course. He was a public-school kid; I went to Holy Names, an all girls' school. I wasn't supposed to go out with him. He was beautiful, though. He knew not to ask me out while he was in high school. He knew the answer, so he waited until he graduated, hoping that would make a difference. It did in time. He was always pleasant as we passed each other, and every few days he would offer to take me on a picnic or on a car ride. In time, I grew to like the idea more and more. He was always there for me. At least back then. Now he is a son of a bitch." She got up to leave the room.

"Sometimes we girls don't know how good we have it. Not even when it is right in front of us."

She kissed me on the back of the head and went to the kitchen to fetch a new bottle of wine, leaving me more confused than before.

It Ends

"Megan has been playing you," Krissy said with half her mouth; the other half was frantically sucking the sweet relief of nicotine from her Marlboro Light.

I toyed with a clove cigarette. It was the smoking equivalent of a pink drink with an umbrella, which happens to be my favorite drink. The fact that I wore sweater vests and sang the entire score of Les Misérables in the car didn't do anything to up my manly quotient.

"How can you say that?"

"She flirted with you to get to another guy; she read your letter professing your love and said nothing; she sat on your lap and played with your hair so she could make some other guy jealous. She is ripping your heart out through your penis. The bitch is heartless."

"Yeah, but she sat on my lap and played with my hair. She smelled like a girl."

"Are guys really that easy to seduce? Are you really that dumb? Are you really led by your penis that much?"

"We aren't led by our penis; it's more of a navigational compass. The dick points us in the right direction, but we still need to drive."

Krissy shook her head in confusion and shame. Throughout the telling of my catastrophic choir trip with Megan she listened intently, pausing only to shake her head side to side in disbelief. "Look," she started, "you're a nice guy with a good heart and a lot of talent and potential. Megan is not your kind of girl. She wants the slick guy, the asshole who will play her games. She has had dolts fall for her all her life."

"So I am a dolt?"

"Sweetie, you aren't good looking enough to pull off dolt. Dolt is a reach for you."

"So what am I?"

"You're more of an imbecile."

"Well that's just great. I come to you with the hopes of feeling better, and I get this."

"Well that'll teach ya."

It was the morning of my high school graduation and weeks had passed since had I poured my heart out on three pages of notebook paper and placed them into Megan's unfeeling hands. She had read them with little emotion, stuck the papers into her pocket, and then reached into my chest cavity and pulled out my still-beating heart. She had cackled like a witch and then bit into my fleshy heart, devouring it so it was one with her toxic body. It was all very East German of her. At least that's how it seemed to me.

I recovered by silently whimpering the rest of the bus ride home while she sat next to me. Sometimes I looked at her chest, as she wasn't wearing a bra and the shocks on the bus were well worn, but that was only to make myself feel better. The knowledge that I would never grasp such breasts only made my grief that much more intense.

I chatted with Becca after the trip. She had been kind enough to call after the prom, but I was so wrapped up in Megan that

I hadn't been very receptive to her advances. Now that Megan was clearly done with me, I was able to focus on Becca. Sure, she was dumb, but she made up for it by being slutty and having low standards. The fact that she appeared to have some serious daddy issues only increased my attraction to her.

On our first date after the prom she came over to try some of my Ritalin. I was truly riddled with ADD. This led to a wonderful drug prescription that, when used as directed, would help with my focus, but when used improperly would lead to great, blackout-style rushes that ended with me weaving through traffic with Becca's robust bra on my head. I knew Becca was likely using me for my Ritalin, but I was using her to get over Megan, so there was no guilt. All's fair in love and war.

The graduation ceremony for Prep took place at the Opera House downtown. It was built to look futuristic but just left the viewer with an uneasy feeling, as if the building had been discarded by an alien craft. It had no clean lines but rather wavy levels that confused the eye. It was built during the World's Fair in 1974 and had been ahead of its time – if by "time" we mean it was piece of crap before its birth. The building was rundown and aged. It had large patches of rust on the outside girders, the interior carpet was a shag orange, and dim mirrors lined the hallways.

The graduates lined up alphabetically down the corridor, waiting to proceed into the ceremony that would effectively end a most revered chapter of their lives. Of course, the real end of the era would take place that night by Angle Lake on a wooded bluff dotted with kegs provided by Walsh's über cool and recently paroled uncle, Titus.

As the procession started, I noticed my dad standing towards the rear of the theater. He gave me a smile and a nod of the head in congratulations. Towards the front of the auditorium I passed my mother and younger brother, Skidmark (not his birth name). Mom wore her fancy mink coat, the one that prompted Mike to ask how many harmless squirrels had to die to make that jacket. She sat with Skidmark devouring a *People* magazine. The ceremony was punctuated with the standard graduation drivel, how this was the time of our life, how we would be friends forever, and any other clichés we could come up with. At no point did anything fun happen, like someone letting off a stink bomb or a streaker running across the auditorium (like Dan had promised).

The best we could muster was when Edmund walked to the stage. He was nicknamed Un-nut because he had only one testicle, which was discovered at homecoming in our sophomore year. He had managed to talk Katie into a closet for a little one-on-one time when she burst through the gym doors shaking her head, flailing her arms as if to fly away, and spitting out of her mouth.

"Uh, gross," was all we got out of her for a few minutes until she told everyone that Edmund only had one love marble. I guess he lost the other in a bout of smallpox as a child. Tragic, but he would have to be ridiculed to the point of suicide, because (naturally) we had no choice.

So, old Un-nut strode onto the stage after his name was called and was greeted by three-quarters of the senior class singing a nifty jingle they had composed on his behalf titled "One Balla." Even the Japanese exchange student, Shota, laughed at poor Edmund. "Only one testicle? In my country, we fall on swords for much less. It shames your family, Edmund." Shota was a little harsh.

Mr. Lock was given the "Teacher of the Year" award and was greeted by a standing ovation from his students and players.

The ceremony was boring and seemed to last forever – mostly because we all wanted to get out of there and up to the lake to start partying. Yet, here we were, as one old person after another droned on. The flip side, of course, was cash. After the ceremony, the students had parties put on by their parents for family and friends to wish good tidings. My mother's Russian housekeeper was working hard to put mine together as we sat there with the blathering adults at the Opera House.

However, to attend a party one must bring gifts, preferably in the form of greenbacks. No one showed up at my party except the housekeeper, my mother, brother, Sam Magee (who simply had no other place to be), and about 400 Russian cheese balls. However, my aunts and uncles had all loaded up the mailbox with guilt-cash for me. It was enough to help get me through the summer stuffed full of wine coolers and fast food. My heart was overwhelmed.

As dusk rolled around, I packed my overnight bag for the evening ahead: a change of clothes, an extra pair of shoes in case I got thrown in the lake, a flashlight in case of monsters, and a sleeping bag for two. The plan was simple; I had laid the groundwork to spend a magical night on the cusp of consciousness with Becca, hopefully climaxing in a night she would spend years of therapy trying to forget. When Mike picked me up for the forty-five-minute journey north to the lake he already had Dan, Andrew, and F-ing Walsh in the car.

"You ready for this? Big night for you," Mike opened.

"What are you talking about?"

"Becca. Tonight's the night, right? You're going to bang her. Lose that cherry of yours."

"You make it sound beautiful."

"Don't worry, it will only last a minute," said Dan.

"Yeah, she won't feel a thing," Mike added.

"I am going to have sex, too, you know," F-ing Walsh said in between spits of chew.

"We know, Walsh, I am sure you are."

"Who's the lucky girl?"

"I don't know yet, but it will be someone. Everyone gets laid on senior campout."

"Well, let's hope it's that easy," I said. "Let's just hope."

The fact was that the senior campout *was* the last good chance of having sex that year. Most guys had mentally already turned the page to the easier, college girl types, but they had this one night to exorcise the demons of girls who left them in the cold in high school. This was the last chance for the unbecoming like myself to win over a girl. This was the last chance for the quiet and reserved girls to throw caution to the wind and be the wild girls they had always dreamed of being. Legend had it that senior campout was the place where good girls became bad, and boys became men. It was to be the night of our lives.

F-ing Walsh added, "Guys I'm really hungry. Can't we pick up some chicken nuggets or something?" F-ing Walsh always had a way of putting things into proper perspective.

We got to the camp as the sun was just arcing across the skyline, lighting the sky with the soft glows of gold and yellow and reflecting off the mirror-smooth lake. The site was already abuzz with activity. A few dozen people had readied

196

the campsite and built a central fire pit for the camp fire, while others simply lounged about with a red plastic cup in hand, never more than a few yards from a keg. Several kegs surrounded the perimeter while other campers brought out coolers full of cheap beer or, worse, Boone's Hill...you know, for the girls...I mean I drink the stuff, but only to try to fit in.

I spotted Megan on the east end of the site. Joe Gaukroger lurked nearby with a red cup in his hand. He had his shirt off and his hairless body glistened in the evening glow. He was magnificent. I wondered how much Crisco he had put on his torso to get that sheen. I set up my tent as far west as possible, hoping that I had beat Becca to the campsite. I wasn't sure if she would bring a tent or just assumed she would bunk with someone. I figured she was planning on being in someone else's tent and I was the fallback plan. The evening was ratcheting up when Becca appeared out of the darkness. She had on tight khaki shorts and a small white tank top that she had cut to just above her naval for maximum effect. The outfit was further enhanced by a push-up bra that caused her breasts to spill out of her top. Her red hair was pulled back, with her trademark sultry curls framing her face. I sat by the campfire flanked by Dan and Andrew when Becca came up to me, planted both of her feet on either side of me, and lowered herself onto my lap. She sat facing me and kissed the bridge of my nose.

"Hi, baby," she said.

"Hi," I responded, my voice cracking. With that she got up and went to find the keg.

"You're gonna have sex tonight?" Andrew said.

"I think I just did. I need to go change my shorts."

I got up to leave and ran into Mike out by the trailhead leading in.

"Mike, what are you doing out here?"

"I am waiting on a couple of girls from North Central."

"You brought girls up here?"

"Sure, all the Prep girls know me. No way they're letting me into their pants."

He had a point. On my walk back I saw F-ing Walsh sharing a cheeseburger with Tania, who was nicknamed Taniatanic because she was roughly the same tonnage as the famous luxury liner. Meanwhile, a minor panic had broken out as some of the drunkards had decided it would be funny to push a girl's Toyota Celica off the bluff. The girl, Erin Broylan, was near a full-blown fit by the time Cody calmed her down.

"Now Erin, don't worry, we'll take care of replacing the car for you. We will all pitch in. An '83 Celica, right? I am sure between all of us we can come up with the forty bucks. Here take a couple of these uppers. It will calm you down."

At the campfire, dancing was in full swing. The stereo from a truck was blasting Green Day, and Becca shook her hips to the music as the fire glowed behind her. Everyone that watched her wished to have a closer look at those hips. They wanted to be me. It was weird – typically, no one wanted to be me, including ME.

I saw her on the fringes at first, just a shadow. She stepped a few feet into the fingers of light that were cast by the fire. Megan had a cup in her hand, and even from my perch I could see that her eyes were glassy from some sort of drug.

She wore a pair of blue jeans with a purple sweater. Her blond hair floated about her shoulders. She didn't sway to the music, she just took in the action from afar, a bystander. It was Andrew who broke my focus on her.

"Oh my God," he announced to the crowd, "F-ing Walsh just went into his tent with Taniatanic."

"Like together, like they might mate?"

"Yeah, they could be bumping uglies right now."

"Holy Shit. We should go listen outside their tent and then mock and jeer."

"Fuck yeah, we should."

With that the mob departed towards F-ing Walsh's four-man tent, which I am sure could barely contain the two of them.

We silently hovered outside the tent listening to the quiet chatter inside.

F-ing Walsh was saying, "If I could be anything, Tania, I would be your tear, to be born in your eye, to live on your cheek, and die on your lips."

The smacking of four fat lips coming together followed this.

"Oh, man, what a terrible line!"

"I can't believe she fell for that."

"How did F-ing Walsh get my line?" exclaimed Joe Gaukroger.

"This is disgusting; I can't listen to this."

"It's like a big flabby train wreck, how can you not?"

After the awkward sucking sound subsided we could make out Tania's salty voice.

"My mama always said that men are like carpet: If you lay them right you can walk on them for years."

More sucking noises and a cheer from the crowd followed. Some raised their glasses as the tent and, truly, the earth, started to rock. It was a 2.3 on the standard Richter scale.

"Am I in?" F-ing Walsh asked. "I can't tell."

"No that's not, that's not it, that's my stomach."

"But it feels like it."

"But it's not; it's lower."

"Nah, I'm gonna stick with this."

Once the urge to vomit subsided, I stumbled back to the fire. There Becca waited for me. It was getting late, and the effects of the booze were taking ahold of most of us. From across the fire I could see Megan sitting on a log with her head in her hands. I knew that look; she was as close to out of it as she got. Joe Gaukroger sat next to her rubbing her shoulders. It wasn't my business, and Becca stole my attention away with a soft kiss. I took Becca's hand into my own and watched the fire crackle and pop. Fing Walsh stumbled into the circle to loud cheers and jeers from the senior class. He smiled.

"Baby," Becca whispered into my ear while she twirled my hair, "do you feel up to going back to your tent?"

"Up to it? I think I have been there twice since you sat down."

"Come with me. I'll take good care of you."

With that she led me out of the circle towards my tent. I knew I was the envy of many of the eyes that were on us. On the other hand, no one could figure out what Becca was doing. I must be dying of an obscure disease, and this was my last wish, they probably thought.

"I haven't done this before," I said.

"I know. Trust me, I know."

"So, you sure you want to hook up with me?"

"Why are you so negative about yourself? You're a sweet guy. You're funny, and kind, and so grateful. I mean, you're really grateful."

"Will you respect me in the morning?" I said taking her into my arms.

"I don't respect you now."

"That's okay, but this needs to be more than sex."

"Yeah, yeah, whatever," she responded.

I allowed myself to explore her with my eyes. She was stunning.

After a few moments, I heard a rustle outside a few hundred yards away. I heard a groan and more commotion.

Then the voices filtered in, crashing my party.

"Hey, get out here!" It was Dan.

"It's going to be a minute at best, Dan. Just wait!"

"Think about baseball and get out here. We need you."

I looked over at Becca. Stunning.

"Be quick," she said.

"Is that really what a girl says to someone during sex?"

"Not until they're married."

Outside the tent Dan, Mike, and Andrew stood with their arms folded.

"We got a problem with Joe Gaukroger," Mike started.

"He broke F-ing Walsh's nose," Andrew added.

"Because he banged a fat chick?"

"No if that was the case he would beat my ass once a month," Mike said.

"F-ing Walsh called him out for pulling Megan into his tent."

"Pulled her into his tent?"

"Yeah, she is way out of it and kept saying "no" under her breath, but he just kept pulling her. F-ing Walsh tried to stop it, and Joe broke his nose."

"Where is she now?"

"In his tent, I guess. F-ing Walsh slowed him, but he didn't deviate from his course."

"Here's your chance," Dan said. "You've been talking about getting a crack at Gaukroger for a long time; well, you're needed."

I had Becca waiting for me in my tent in a state of undress, and yet I was contemplating pulling Megan, a girl who had mercilessly stomped on my heart, out of the biggest bully in school's tent.

"What about Becca?" I asked.

"Don't worry; I'll take care of her," Mike assured me.

"No way, you guys are coming with me. I could use the back up. Andrew, get F-ing Walsh and meet me outside Joe's tent."

I started to stride toward the offending tent on the east end of the campground. A full moon lit the path. The treetops swayed gently in the night breeze. I could feel the adrenaline of the moment start to kick in. It had been awhile since I had been in a true fight. Not since the Academy. I hadn't always faired so well in those fights, but I had fought my share of Joe Gaukrogers. I counted on them under estimating me. You didn't break my friend's nose and you didn't pull Megan into a tent with you against her will. There was something about having a level of class. The fact that my erection was only just now subsiding seemed to argue against my point, but we can gloss over that.

I could feel the eyes of my classmates on me as I neared the tent. My boys followed close behind, and something told me that this was my moment. I wasn't going to allow myself to be put down and put away. Joe couldn't just take what he wanted; someone had to put him in his place. He couldn't break a guy's nose for raising his voice to him, and he couldn't bully people to keep them in fear. "This ends tonight," I told myself.

"Joe, get out here!" I yelled at his tent.

"Go away, shit bag."

"Get out here before I drag your ass out."

With that I could hear some rustling and the shaking of the tent as Joe Gaukroger, sans shirt, burst through the nylon flaps of the tent. His eyes fixed on me, then burned through me.

"What the fuck do you think you're doing? Who do you think you're talking to?"

He poked me hard in the chest with his finger. Megan pulled herself from the tent and threw up.

"You know Joe, I've met guys just like you. You're a talker. Talkers always seem to be on the fringes of a fight. Talking about how tough they are, what a badass they are. But they are always just talk. You see, I'm the other kind of guy. I don't say much. I don't look for a fight, but when it lands on my doorstep, I do what has to be done. You punched my friend. You pulled a semi-conscious girl into your tent, and, well, you're a dick. I can't stand for that." I had practiced the speech in my head for several minutes. Nailed it.

"Oh, is that right?" he asked, poking my chest again.

The memories of the past flooded back to me. He had stolen my girl at the football game, he had challenged me in front of my friends, he had slapped me, and I did nothing but cower. "Joe, don't touch me again."

"Yeah, why not?" He poked my chest again. With my left hand, I grabbed his two fingers and quickly twisted and broke them.

He let out a howl of pain and glanced around the circle that had formed. He was looking for allies. None appeared. He was bigger than me. Grappling with him would be a mistake. I needed to find a way to neutralize his bulk. I had poked the bear, and I needed a strategy.

I was full of fear. Courage isn't a lack of fear but a respect and mastery of the fear. Mr. Lock had spoken of it in football, and I had taken the idea to heart. I needed to remain sharp and master the fear that now bubbled to the surface and threatened to overcome me.

Angry, Joe turned his broad shoulders back to me. The two fingers that I had broken were on his right hand, and that left him with only his left. He swung wildly, and I sidestepped easily. By now a crowd had gathered, forming a circle around us. Joe bull-rushed me, swinging his arms in a windmill as he did. He was hoping to land something, or at least take me with his mass. As he rushed towards me, I sidestepped and fell to one knee. With my right hand, I punched the side of his kneecap with all my might, dislocating it. He fell to the ground like a sack of bricks, clutching his leg and whimpering.

With that, the fight was over. Joe couldn't walk. The crowd dispersed excitedly, ready to see what would happen next that night. I scanned for Megan. I spotted her a few yards away, her head in the grass. She was once again expelling her insides. I gently pulled her hair back and let the sickness wash through her.

"Feeling any better?"

"No."

"You got a tent?"

"That blue one."

Her tent was only a few feet away. I pulled her to it and gently helped her inside.

"Thanks," she said.

I tucked her into her sleeping bag.

"No problem, just get some sleep."

"Why are you always there for me?"

"I've told you. I love you, or I think I do. I am not going to let anything happen to you, least of all a Neanderthal like Joe."

"Who uses words like Neanderthal? That's why I thought you were gay."

"You thought I was gay?"

"Sure, we all do – the sweater vests, the show tunes. You never hooked up with girls; all our gay-dars were on high alert. Why did you think I always flirted with you?"

"Because I'm not gay?"

"Your mouth says 'no,' but your knowledge of Miss Saigon says 'yes.'"

"Hey, I almost had sex with Becca tonight."

"Everyone has almost had sex with Becca; that's not proof you're not gay."

"I am not gay."

"I am not judging. Either way, thanks for your help and always being there for me."

"Sure thing, just get to sleep." I turned to leave.

"Where are you going?"

"Back to my tent."

"Can you just stay with me tonight? Just for a while anyhow?"

What was I doing? My penis and my heart were in a death dance. My penis said go, go to the sure thing, but my heart was with Megan. In the end, I followed my heart. I know – gay, right?

"Okay, I can stay."

She opened the sleeping bag and pulled it back to allow me in. I kicked off my shoes and climbed inside. She wrapped the bag and her arms around me.

"I'm leaving tomorrow."

"We're all leaving tomorrow. We're in a grass field"

"No, I am *leaving*, leaving."

"Where are you going?" I asked.

"To LA. I know some people there who think they can get me a chance to sing."

"What about school?"

"I hate school. I just want to sing and get as far away from here as I can. I can't stand my life. I can't stand me. I need to get a fresh start. You should come with me."

"I have college to go to."

"Hell, you can go to community college in LA. Come live with me. We will do this together. You have to live in the moment. There isn't a tomorrow for us. There is just this moment and what it means. What if a bus hit you? Have you done all that you hoped to do? Have you kissed all the girls you hoped to and written the songs you wanted? I want to go to LA. I want to live. I want to party and sing and just be. I hate waiting. I have to live like today is my last. I have to. Come with me. Live with me. It's unbelievably freeing when you do everything without regard to what it might mean."

With that she kissed me. Her breath was horrible. I mean, she had just vomited.

"Okay," I said. "If you want, I'll go with you."

My heart leapt. I mean, if I was going to pass on sex with Becca for Megan – dropping out of college, disappointing my family, and disowning my friends was *nothing*.

"We leave on the Greyhound bus at 10:00 A.M." I could feel her smile. I felt like my whole life was about to begin.

She wrapped me tighter in her arms and then I could hear her gentle snore.

The next morning, I woke with a start. I could hear the subtle activity of drunken youth outside. Megan was gone. Her car was gone. It was only 8:30, but if we were really leaving at 10:00 I had precious little time to get to my stuff and get to the bus stop. I grabbed her tent but left my own as I discovered Becca and both F-ing Walsh and Johnson in the tent with her. Both sets of legs stuck out of the door of the tent. I hope they hadn't crossed swords. I didn't have a ride. I pulled Mike out of his tent.

"I need your car."

"No way."

"Please, Mike."

"I am not giving you my Chevy Nova. It's a classic for God's sake."

"It's a classic piece of shit. The front side has a spring that pokes up every time you hit a bump. It's more effective than the morning after pill. I am begging you, please."

He sighed.

"Okay, I'll drive you. God, you're a bitch."

We hit the road and arrived at my house at 9:30. I strolled past my mother and packed a quick duffel bag that would have to last me the rest of my life. I was so excited that I even stopped to say good-bye to my mom. I grabbed the wad of graduation cash. Hopefully it was enough to get me a ticket and set the two of us up in a place. I would need to call my dad and figure out the rest as I went. This felt like the craziest thing I had ever done.

"Mike, can you take me to the bus station?"

Without a word, he pulled out of the driveway and by 9:55 I had a ticket in hand and boarded the bus. I looked in vain for Megan. She was nowhere to be found. I retraced my steps and looked everywhere in the terminal for her, even the women's room where I found a very angry bag lady in the midst of her morning routine.

I watched as the bus slowly pulled away. Dumbfounded, I sat on the bench outside of the bus station. I looked out at the fresh summer morning. My whole life was ahead of me, and the one thing I wanted was nowhere to be seen. I sat quietly, lost in my thoughts for a moment, and didn't notice Mike take the seat next to me.

"She's gone," he said.

"Sure seems that way."

"I have no idea why you're surprised."

"You would think I would know."

"I think Gaukroger is going to sue you. He can't walk. Had to go the hospital."

"Good, he is a piece of shit."

"So…she gave me this to give to you." Mike produced a letter.

"When did she give this to you?"

"This morning. She woke me up and told me to give it to you."

"You're just telling me this now?"

"Yeah, it was a lot more fun watching you twist in the wind. You should have seen your face. Oh, I am so sad and lost without her. Ha! It was priceless." What an ass.

I caressed the carefully folded corners of the note. My name was scribbled in the cursive I knew so well across the front. I was disgusted. Who tells someone how they feel in a note, anyhow?

> *I didn't have the heart to wake you this morning. I hope you will understand and forgive me. I wanted so badly for you to come with me, to be with me. You have no idea how much I love you, have always loved you. From the first time I kissed you in Laura's basement I knew you were the boy I would compare all others to. That is why I must leave without you. The fact that on a second's notice you would come with me to LA just proves that you are too good for me. I am no good for you, and in time you will grow tired of me, and you will move on. I can't lose you like that. At least this way we have some mystery left, and when I get it together and if it times up*

right, we will find each other like you hoped. It kills
me to write this. I know that you are the best thing
for me, but I love you enough to know that I am the
worst thing for you. You wrote in your letter that
you would always have a place in your heart for me
and that you would dream of me. Keep me in your
heart and dream of me often, and maybe someday
both our dreams will come true.

Love, Megan

My shoulders sunk and my gut felt like it had just taken a body blow from Mike Tyson. I couldn't believe how much it hurt. My mind raced to my favorite moment with Megan. It was after school, and I was down in the choir room. Mr. Lock puttered in the back of the room filing away sheet music while I played the piano. It was a nice piece I had written, slow moving with a distant hope in the chords. Megan quietly walked in the room and sat as I tinkered. She was in that familiar state where she was sad and lost, but held the flame of hope inside. She watched me and then stood by the piano. She tried on a shy, self-conscious smile and she quietly sang along to the music I was playing. The words were not completed, just syllables as her mind folded into the music. Her body pressed against the piano, and her eyes closed slowly. She rocked gracefully and seductively to the music. When I stopped playing, she held those eyes closed for a minute and then slowly turned her head to look down at me, ripping at my eyes. She held them firm as if there was no other man in the world who could understand her like I did in that moment.

"Did you read this?" I asked Mike.

"Yup."

"What do you think?"

"I feel bad for you. Should have tried to sleep with her last night."

"I guess so."

"Sorry, buddy," Mike said. "Tell you what. Take my sister."

"I don't want Krissy."

"Oh, come on, I want you to."

We walked out with his arm around me towards his car.

"No one wants your fucking sister, and don't touch me."

"I hear she's pretty good..."

The Final Phone Call

I was just walking towards the bedroom after a late-night episode of COPS. Watching COPS made me feel better about my loved ones and myself, but not by much. It was late, but not yet past midnight, when the phone rang. I picked up the receiver and greeted my old dream, Megan, again.

"Hi," she said in a soft, gentle voice. I could feel her trepidation through the phone.

"Hello. I wondered if I would hear from you again."

"Sorry about all of this. It's just…I don't have anyone else to call. I'm not sure anyone else would be willing to listen."

I turned off the TV and sat in my living room and listened to my pounding heartbeat. Even in this stage of my life I could hear the thundering of my nervous heart in my ears. My palms were moist and my breath jagged.

"I can listen," I said.

"I am leaving tomorrow and starting over."

"How will you start over?"

"I am not sure. I guess I will do as I am told and just take it a day at a time. I really can't worry about tomorrow. All I have is today. Today I am sober. Today I am content and centered, and today I am happy."

"When was the last time you could say that? That you were happy?"

"I can't even remember. I know I was once. I remember what it feels like to truly laugh and have fun and be admired; I just can't recall when I felt it last. But I will again. I am determined."

I had seen this before in my dad – the bottom, the dark abyss, and the power of the rebirth. It takes time. Sometimes it takes many attempts and some never shake the demons. The best moments were the ones when the addict found the steely resolve and power to truly believe they could defeat it. The worst, of course, was the crushing desperation when once again the addict failed. Sure, I had seen this before, and I had also seen it work. It took the immense strength of sitting down and living in the moment and having the power to say "no" to your shadows and desires in that moment. The second you thought of the days ahead it could break you. It cascades on you like a tidal wave. All the weight of who you were and the sum of your life up to that point pulls you down like a stiff undertow, and you could be lost forever. Sure, I had seen this before, and what my friend needed now was hope, the most powerful and elusive of emotions.

Hope controls our life. Some have it and others have given it up, but hope shapes us. I spent so much time lying in my bed at night picturing Megan with only the hope that someday she would love me like I loved her. It hurt to think that I may not have her, but as long as I had some level of hope that maybe she would find a way to love me then that was enough to keep going. When I extinguished that flame it was so very dark. Megan had lost that ember many years ago. It had been snuffed out. Now she battled again to relight that wick, to find the hope that she once again could live a normal life, without fear, without drugs, without the constant sale of her soul. To nurture that flame it had to be tended in the moment. There was no future.

"I need a favor," she asked. "I don't know anyone else to call. I can't call my family. I don't have the strength yet to talk to them alone. I have no friends left. I just have you."

I took a deep breath. What an odd way to finally feel needed by her.

"Sure. What?"

"Can you pick me up in the morning? Maybe take me to coffee and help me to figure out how I am going to go home?"

I picked her up in front of a large campus of brick buildings that looked like they could have been part of an office park if they hadn't tried so hard to build gardens. The landscape had many flowers, benches, and paths, and it included a man-made waterfall that felt terribly out of place. The lot was just off a busy highway, making the serene Japanese-style gardens feel forced.

She sat on the front steps of the large building with her cheek resting on her balled hand. She had a small duffel bag containing her meager belongings resting beside her. She didn't let go of the handle, as though someone might try to take it from her at any moment. She wore a white sleeveless turtleneck and a pair of jeans that wrapped her body. She had simple makeup on that was obviously her first attempt in a while to look elegant. Her once full strawberry hair was now thin and a dull, muddled brown; her arms were frail, and her once thin, taut body looked malnourished. Her eyes were sunken so that her face looked slightly gaunt. Her body now featured a few harsh tattoos that echoed her past. As I looked at her my throat caught, and I found a nervous metallic taste in my mouth. She was still my Megan. She would always be beautiful to me.

As soon as I stepped out of the car that same old smile that could bring me to my knees played across her lips. What I wouldn't do to evoke that smile. She picked up her bag and slowly walked towards me. When we found each other, she dropped that bag and reached up on her toes to wrap her arms around me in the warmest embrace I had ever felt from her. It came from a place of true need. I took her bag, and she took my hand as we walked to the car.

Once in the car she didn't say anything, just reached to turn up the air conditioning. It made the tips of her hair dance on her shoulders. We didn't speak for several moments. I drove to her childhood home. I didn't need directions. We pulled up in front of the old house and I turned off the car. It was only then that she turned to address me.

"You told me you would always be here for me."

"I always meant it."

"You're married now?"

"I am."

"I hear you have a daughter?"

"Yeah, terrifying, huh?"

"For both of you." She giggled.

"Are you happy?" she asked.

"Yes," I answered.

She didn't say anything; she just sat in the car.

"Do you want me to go with you?" I asked.

"No. You have done enough. I just need a second to get my nerves together."

I looked over at the house. The front curtains slyly opened and revealed an old set of eyes. They looked into the front seat of the car.

"You're the only one who ever really cared about me. I wish I had loved you when I knew how important it was."

"I will always love you Megan. There will always be room in my heart for you."

She opened the door then leaned over to hug me one last time. She grabbed both sides of my face and buried her eyes in mine. No words were needed. She grabbed the small duffel bag that was her life and slowly walked up to the steps of her former home. The curtains fluttered closed, and, before Megan could even fully gather herself to knock, the door opened to reveal the weathered face of her mother. Megan's eyes were firmly planted on the ground but eventually found her mothers' when her mother grabbed her by the shoulders and looked into her daughter's face. It was then that she pulled her child to her, and all was forgiven. Such is the way of unconditional love. There is always a place for a fresh start.

Megan looked back at me and smiled before she walked into her home.

I truly loved Megan. The thing with love is that each love is separate and delicate. I love my wife. She is the best thing to ever happen to me. To love Megan doesn't make me love her less. Our hearts can hold more love then we can ever give. What made our love strong is that it was forged in longing and misses. There was no judgment. Sure, maybe some regret, but not on my part. Not being with Megan was likely the best thing that happened to me. The path I ended on led to my wife and my daughter. I wouldn't trade that. What was left was unconditional. I was there for her, just like I promised. To love unconditionally is to see the shadow of God, even, and maybe especially, if it isn't reciprocated.

Upon Reflection

The best thing that ever happened to me may have been that missed bus. I was so elated at the time, thinking of living with Megan, of finally having Megan – that I was blinded to what was the best thing for me. In my entire relationship with Megan up to that moment, she had never made a decision that put my feelings ahead of her own. In that way, her decision to mislead me and leave early was a first step in her maturation as a person. LA would kick her ass, and she found herself more alone than ever. She could have used me to lean on and she knew it, but not wanting to lead me further down a road that clearly was a dead end was a kind gesture on her part. For me it marked the true end of youth and helped me to embark on my future as a college student.

That night I said goodbye to my lifelong friends, knowing that much would change. We would no longer be able to rely on each other for support every day. We would be forced to leave the nest and rediscover the world with fresh eyes.

Mike would pull his shit together and go on to grad school and become a city planner. Dan would remain a mystery man. He became a blues drummer in a band. He would go on to bang most of the women in town and still find time to graduate with top grades in college. I am not sure how he found the time for studying, music, and countless bouts of sex. Do I sound jealous? Like all of us he would have to face his demons in trying to find his true core. The coke didn't help.

Andrew would go on to make a living in bariatric sales – that is the sale of medical equipment to the chronically obese. He made good money and claimed I inspired him. He is still an asshole – no amount of fat people money has changed that.

F-ing Walsh might someday use some of Andrew's equipment. Of all of us, he grew to become the most put together. He married a girl well out of his league, or what I like to call, the dream. She bore him two children, a matching set. F-ing Walsh took over his father's company and could now own us all. We resent him for his success but still use his lake cabin whenever allowed.

We still see each other from time to time – at weddings, reunions, and once when bailing one of the guys out of a Las Vegas jail cell for solicitation. It's always the same bond that connected us as kids. Each time we meet it's as if time has not moved since we last saw each other. True friendship has the lasting power of Styrofoam. We know the best of each other and, of course, over time we have learned the shortcomings. History is the glue of such friendships. Those childhood friends become more like brothers. In the end, you know you can count on them.

Laura would grow up to have a mildly attractive, but dull-as-paint husband who sold life insurance. She would grow a belly and be content to teach grade school and allow her suppleness to spread across her desk chair. All-in-all she was simple and wildly happy with her life.

Katie would graduate college and soon after find herself pregnant. Not sure which man had fathered the spawn, she accused all of them and some others, too. Just to see what stuck. You can't fight DNA and soon enough she found herself with not only a bassinet but also a ring. I wasn't invited to the wedding.

Krissy remained around via Mike.

Some people have a charmed life and never really understand it. They float through existence with a certain level of grace and beauty and do not know they have that grace and beauty. Because of that they are even more illuminating to those of us with dark corners in our souls. Sometimes these people are able to shine their bright and blinding light into these dark corners, and, at least in their presence, give us a simple joy that we cannot seem to capture without them. They shine a light on all of the joy we possess. Our time with them is filled with laughter and hope. The time flies by when we are with them as all good things go, too fast. I have known a few of these people throughout my life. I have never been able to keep them as close to me as I wanted. Often this type of person burns hot. They have so much passion for life that they scold to the touch. These people move from place to place and adventure to adventure and discard people in their midst. Those discarded shrivel from the cold that is left; where once we lived in the light and heat they generated. The world became a little grayer and bleaker without them. We are their victims, left to cope with a world that has lost some color. We hold onto the memory of the warm glow. We cherish the photos and memories that we shared together, and for a few moments we can warm those dark corners in our souls when we look through those old photos. But alas, these are empty silos compared to the actual moments.

Those who bring the light have a huge amount of energy and power, but often crash harder than the rest of us. They burn out. It takes a huge amount of energy to live at their wavelength, and sometimes that passion is turned inwards. They focus on themselves and that can bring a certain level of disaster because this person does not bother to recognize the beauty that they possess. It never registers how much they mean to others, so that when they crash they feel totally alone and lost. They plunge into the darkness that most have learned to cope with, accept, and some to even embrace. This is foreign to those with the gift of light, and the darkness is a cave of fears and loss for them. If they do not have a rock of a person to pick them up and hold them, they fall forever into the cave of eternal night. The crushing black of doubt and ridicule silences their fragile light. Their fragile existence that seemed so beautiful and bright may play like the rock of Gibraltar but in fact is a house built on sand. That is why for the light to burn it must have a caretaker, someone to tend the fire. For those who do not have this, their light and warmth is gone far too soon, making the world a much sadder place to exist.

Megan was one of these people of light. I loved her brilliance and always hoped she would return the love and light my soul on fire. In the end, I guess it was up to me to caretake my own fire.

Made in the USA
San Bernardino, CA
03 December 2018